The Art of
Passover

The Art of
Passover

Compiled and edited by

Rabbi Stephan O. Parnes

With essays by

Bonni-Dara Michaels and Gabriel M. Goldstein

UNIVERSE

Published by Universe Publishing
A Division of Rizzoli International Publications, Inc.
300 Park Avenue South
New York, NY 10010
www.rizzoliusa.com

Designer: Ken Scaglia
Photo Research: Ellin Yassky
Editorial Production: Diane Lawrence

2016 2017 2018 2019 / 10 9 8 7 6 5 4 3 2 1

Printed in China

ISBN-13: 978-0-7893-3118-2

Library of Congress Catalog Control Number: 2015952074

Frontispiece:
Afikomen Pouch. China. 19th Century.
Cotton, satin, embroidery thread, gold thread.
Diameter: 5¾ in. (14.6 cm.)
Hebrew Union College Skirball Museum, Los Angeles.

Contents

PREFACE
Rabbi Stephan O. Parnes   7

INTRODUCTION
Bonni-Dara Michaels
Gabriel M. Goldstein   8

SOUTHERN GERMANY
The Birds' Head Haggadah   18

SPAIN
Barcelona Haggadah   20

SPAIN
Golden Haggadah   22

CATALONIA
Rylands Sefardic Haggadah   24

GERMANY
Darmstadt Haggadah   26

GERMANY, MIDDLE RHINE
Hamburg Miscellany   28

GERMANY, MIDDLE RHINE
Erna Michael Haggadah   30

GERMANY
Ashkenazi Haggadah   32

ITALY
Rothschild Miscellany   34

ITALY
Passover Haggadah Roundels   36

IRAN
The Book of Exodus   38

MORAVIA
Prague Haggadah   40

CENTRAL EUROPE
Miniature Haggadah   42

ISRAEL
Raban Haggadah   44

UNITED STATES
Ben Shahn Haggadah   46

ALSACE (?)
Passover Banner   48

EUROPE, WESTERN ASHKENAZIC
Ceremonial Towel   50

ALSACE, FRANCE/SOUTHERN GERMANY
Seder Towel   52

ROMANIA/EASTERN EUROPE
Embroidered Matzah Bags   54

GERMANY
Matzah Bag   56

CHINA
Afikomen Pouch   58

ROMANIA/MORAVIA
Embroidered Matzah Bags   60

SPAIN
Lusterware Passover Plate 62

CENTRAL EUROPE (?)
Pewter Passover Plate 64

HUNGARY
Passover Plates 66

ITALY
Majolica Seder Plate 68

JERUSALEM
Brass Seder Plate 70

POLAND
Tiered Seder Set 72

VIENNA
Silver Tiered Seder Plate 74

VIENNA
Repoussé Tiered Seder Plate 76

FRIEDRICH ADLER
Tiered Seder Plate and Elijah Cup 78

ALOIS WÖRLE
Seder Plate 80

TEREZÍN
Terezín Seder Plate 82

LORELEI AND ALEX GRUSS
Tiered Seder Plate:
From Slavery to Freedom 84

GERMANY
Beaker 86

WARSAW
Silver Gilt Goblet 88

GERMANY
Ivory Beaker 90

GERMANY
Glass Goblets 92

MICHEL SCHWARTZ
Cup of Elijah 94

ISTANBUL
Ewer and Basin 96

BERNARD PICART
Search for Leaven / L'Examen du Levain 98

EL LISSITZKY
The Fire Came and Burnt the Stick 100

ARTHUR SZYK
Passover 102

REUVEN RUBIN
First Seder in Jerusalem 104

MARC CHAGALL
Exodus 106

TOBY KNOBEL FLUEK
Making Haroset 108

LARRY RIVERS
History of Matzah 110

ITALY
Omer Calendar 112

INDEX 115

PHOTO CREDITS 119

Preface

The celebration of a special event requires that the event be distinguished from ordinary events. Special attire may be donned and special food may be prepared. Artists and crafters who produce objects for the event will look for ways to refine these objects so that they might be not only functional but also attractive. Certainly the celebration of an important holiday requires the best goods and the best—and most beautiful—clothing and utensils that one has. *Hiddur mitzvah,* the beautification of the performance of a commandment, is a concept that has long been present in the Jewish tradition. The Book of Exodus reports that Moses sang "This is my God, and I will glorify Him." This phrase has been understood in rabbinic literature to mean that one should make one's ritual objects beautiful as a tribute to God.

This book is a celebration of the art that celebrates Passover. The objects and paintings that appear herein were created over the course of more than half a millennium and come from many of the lands in which the Jewish people dwelled. They were selected for their beauty, as well as to represent various media from many times and places. Beauty, however, takes many forms. The beauty of some items, such as the seder plate from Terezín, stems from or is enhanced by the context in which they were created. Limitations of space made it necessary to leave out a great many beautiful and important items. Other items were not available because time and weather, and persecution and war have robbed us of many of the beautiful creations of past centuries—and even of past decades. That as much as we have has survived is testimony to how important these items were to their owners.

The work of an artist gives us a gift that is greater than the physical beauty of the object he or she creates. When an artist creates an object we are presented with another way of seeing that object and what it stands for. We are given the gift of seeing a familiar object as though it were new. This gift assists us in fulfilling the principle set forth in the haggadah that the more we discuss the going out of Egypt the more praiseworthy we are. The works contained in this book can help us to see Passover as it was seen by many Jews through the ages. When new perspectives are offered, the story will endure. Passover always remains to be discovered and understood anew.

Rabbi Stephan O. Parnes

Introduction

The desire to create and use beautiful objects to celebrate the Passover festival is deeply rooted in Jewish tradition and stems from a variety of sources. The experience of the Exodus from Egypt and the transformation from slavery to freedom commemorated at Passover are central to Jewish experience and identity, and it is natural that these themes would be presented in Jewish artistic expression throughout the millennia.

The creation of objects to beautify the celebration of Jewish ritual is known as *hiddur mitzvah* (the beautification of the commandment). The rabbis interpreted a verse from the "Song of the Sea": "this is my God, and I will *glorify* Him" (Exodus 15:2). The Hebrew word *anvehu,* here translated as "glorify," literally means "beautify." In the *Mekhilta,* Rabbi Ishmael asks: "Is it possible for flesh and blood to beautify the Creator?" In the Babylonian Talmud (*Masekhta de-shirah, parashah* 3), *anvehu* is interpreted as: "Make a beautiful sukkah in His honor, a beautiful shofar, beautiful *tsitsit* (ritual fringes), a beautiful Torah scroll written with fine ink and a fine reed by a skilled scribe and wrap it about with beautiful silks."(*Shabbat* 133b). The rabbis therefore taught that the Bible calls on Jews to enhance the observance of ritual commandments through the use of beautiful ceremonial objects and "to become beautiful by fulfilling commandments in a special way." (*Mekhilta, Masekhta de-shirah, parashah* 3).

The earliest known Jewish representation of the Exodus is found in the wall paintings of the third-century Dura Europos synagogue discovered in 1932. Dura Europos was a Roman garrison town in what is now Syria. The synagogue was decorated with elaborate paintings depicting the biblical narrative in a stylistic hybrid of Greco-Roman, Mesopotamian, Parthian, and Sassanian styles. The Exodus story is depicted in many scenes on the west wall, including portrayals of the finding of Moses, the departure from Egypt, and the crossing of the Red Sea. Dura Europos is the only surviving extensive visual representation of the Bible predating the fifth century and suggests to many scholars that later Christian depictions of the biblical narrative stem from a long existing Jewish artistic tradition.

The haggadah provides the structure of the seder service and recounts the story of the Exodus. The earliest known illustrated haggadah is a ninth- or tenth-century manuscript found in fragmentary form in the Cairo *genizah,* a repository for discarded or worn sacred writings. The production of illustrated haggadahs has remained popular until today and has been one of the main vehicles for Jewish artistic creativity and expression. The reasons behind the popularity of haggadah illustration parallel the nature of the seder itself. The seder's primary purpose is to tell and teach the history of the Exodus from Egypt. Illustrations heighten the didactic character of the haggadah's text and bring the narative to life. The seder is structured to entertain and involve children, with food, special questions, and playful songs. The illustrations in haggadahs surely engaged children at seder tables throughout the centuries and helped teach the Passover story.

Haggadah illustrations generally include many representations of human figures. The second

Israelites Crossing the Red Sea. Wall painting, Dura Europos Synagogue, Syria. Third century C.E.

commandment against graven images has been variously construed over the centuries, and rabbinic interpretation and popular practice have frequently been influenced by local non-Jewish custom. Rabbis, patrons, and artists were probably more comfortable with figural representations in haggadahs since these texts were used in home ritual and not in synagogue services, where the suggestion of idolatrous character was more likely.

Throughout the medieval period, beautiful illuminated manuscript haggadahs were created by masterful scribes and artists. The style of illuminated Hebrew manuscripts was basically reflective of contemporary schools of manuscript production in each epoch and region. The text of the haggadah underwent many recensions during the early Middle Ages. Until the thirteenth century the haggadah was generally incorporated as a component of a larger liturgical text. At that time, the interest in producing and commissioning haggadahs was stimulated by developments in European book production. In the thirteenth century, secular manuscript workshops became more prevalent and new forms of books, such as the Christian Book of Hours for private devotion, were commissioned by patrons. Commissions for

luxurious manuscripts multiplied, and scribal workshops increasingly produced comparatively small books for private ownership. In this climate, the production of illuminated haggadahs thrived.

The illustrations of the Passover haggadah can be divided into four categories, paralleling the themes of the seder and the haggadah text: textual (accurate depictions of the haggadah text); ritual (portrayals of the seder service); biblical (depictions of the biblical narrative, primarily, but not exclusively, the account of the Exodus); and eschatological (scenes referring to Israel's ultimate destiny and to the Messianic era). Spanish haggadahs are famed for their richly decorated full-page miniatures, while the haggadahs of the German school feature few full-page illustrations and profuse marginal illustrations. Italian haggadahs follow the Ashkenazic format of marginal illustrations and initial-word panels. Immigrant scribes and artists, such as Joel ben Simeon who moved from Germany to Italy, spread local styles and created new hybrid artistic traditions.

The invention of printing in the fifteenth century inspired new creativity in haggadah illustration. Several pages of the first illustrated printed haggadah, dating from the late fifteenth or early sixteenth century, have survived. This book was either printed in Spain before 1492 or was published by Sefardic refugees in Constantinople after the expulsion of the Jews from Spain. An important illustrated haggadah was published by Gershom and Gronem Cohen in Prague in 1526, featuring more than sixty woodcut illustrations and magnificent woodcut borders surrounding the text. The *Mantua Haggadah* of 1560 was printed from woodblocks, rather than movable type, and includes Italian Renaissance elements such as a depiction of a seated Wise Son resembling Michelangelo's Jeremiah of the Sistine Chapel ceiling. In 1609 the *Venice Haggadah* was printed in three issues with translations in Judeo-Italian, Judeo-German, and Judeo-Spanish to meet the varying linguistic needs of the Italian, Ashkenazic, and Sefardic members of Venice's Jewish community. The illustrations of the *Venice Haggadah* were highly innovative, including the first composite arrangements of scenes depicting the various stages of the seder and the ten plagues. The *Amsterdam Haggadah* of 1695 features delicate, detailed copper engravings by the proselyte Avram bar Ya'akov based on the biblical illustrations of Matthew Merian the elder of Basle (1593–1650). The *Amsterdam Haggadah* included a pull-out map, and its illustrations were widely copied in later haggadahs.

In the eighteenth century, the art of the Hebrew illustrated manuscript haggadah flourished, experiencing a revival after the invention of printing. These manuscripts were primarily commissioned by wealthy Jews, many of whom functioned as court officials. These manuscript haggadahs were frequently modeled on printed editions; scribes imitated the forms of printed letters and page compositions, and artists frequently based their illustrations on printed models. The word "Amsterdam" was prominently placed on the title page of many eighteenth-century haggadah manuscripts, indicating that the text was written in Hebrew letters of the same high quality as the typography of Amsterdam's presses. Most of the surviving examples of eighteenth-century manuscript haggadahs come from Germany, Austria, and Moravia. Scribes and artists copied printed models, but imbued their manuscripts with inventive additions and adaptations.

The Passover table is resplendent with symbolic images. Traditionally, in order to maintain the separation between leavened and unleavened foods, special dishes and utensils are reserved for use only at Passover, or utensils used year round are specially prepared for Passover use. Preparing handmade matzah required special utensils. After the matzah was rolled, it was perforated with a comb or rake-like implement to prevent the dough from rising during baking. The *reidel*, a wheel with sharp teeth attached to a handle, could also be used for this purpose. It was run across the matzah in lines crossing at right angles. Some bakers may have used a compass to ensure that the matzah was uniform in size and to trim the edges neatly. In 1875 a machine for matzah production was made in England. Since it was easier to produce machine-made matzah in squares, the traditional circular matzah was gradually replaced.

The very table setting for the Passover meal recalls the special meaning of the festival and reiterates the

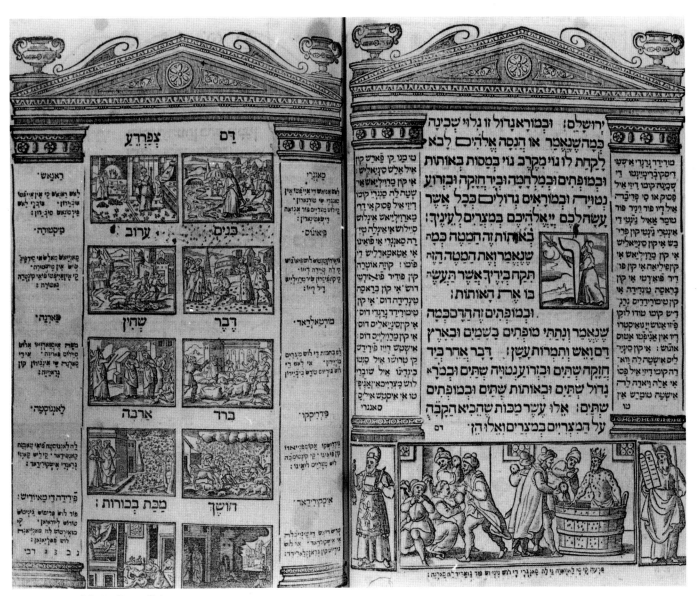

Venice Haggadah, Ladino edition, 1609.
Ink on vellum.
11 ⅛ × 7 ⅝ in. (28.3 × 19.4 cm).
Moldovan Family Collection.

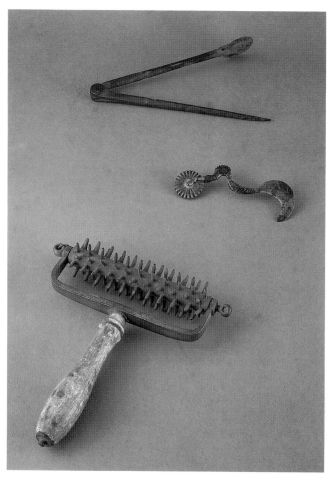

Eighteenth-century tools used for handmade matzah.
Top to bottom: Compass, *reidel,* perforating roller.
The Jewish Museum, New York.

Exodus story. Passover foods, free of leaven, add to
the symbolism at every Passover meal. At the seder,
the symbolism is accentuated. Symbolic foods such as
the *karpas* (green vegetable), *maror* (bitter herbs),
and matzah are displayed and eaten. Specially crafted
vessels to hold the ceremonial foods enhance the
symbolism of these foods. A seder plate bearing
ceremonial foods is placed at the center of the table.
Often these plates are tiered to hold the three
matzahs, emphasizing the significance of the unleavened bread. The tiered plates hold sets of small vessels
for the ceremonial foods. These vessels were often
created to signify the meaning of the foods eaten at
the seder. *Haroset,* a sweet mixture often made of
apples, nuts, and wine, symbolizes the mortar used
by the slaves in Egypt and was often presented at
the seder table in a container shaped like a wheelbarrow. The use of beautiful utensils at the seder
evokes the freedom celebrated at Passover. Yosef Caro
(1488–1575) states in his famed Code of Jewish Law,
the *Shulhan Arukh,* that one should "set their table
[for the Passover seder] with beautiful vessels . . . in
the manner of freedom" (*Orah Hayyim* 472:2). Only
free men have the ability to own and enjoy beautiful
objects, and the beautification of the seder table is in
itself an assertion of freedom.

The various stages of the seder service are
enhanced by the use of ornamental objects. Ewers,
basins, and towels are used for the ritual handwashing
before eating the green vegetable and the matzah.
Decorated Passover towels are frequently displayed in
the home throughout the festival. Pillowcases adorn
the pillows used to recline at the seder, a symbol

of prosperity and freedom. Elegant vessels for the four cups of wine and for Elijah's cup grace the seder table. Covers or bags for the matzahs also heighten, and even explain, the symbolism. They are often embellished with embroidered inscriptions referring to Passover as "the festival of matzahs" or with the blessing recited before eating the matzah. Tabs on each of the three compartments label the matzahs as Kohen, Levi, and Israel, the three divisions of Jewish people, defining the symbolic nature of the three covered ceremonial matzahs. In many communities, special bags were made for storing and hiding the *afikomen.* Often, preexisting pieces were adapted to be used for this purpose, such as the embroidered bag from China. While matzah bags were created expressly for the seder, they were made using contemporary needlework techniques and motifs.

In every epoch and locale, Jews adopted customs from the general population and adapted regional esthetics and culture to create a distinct local Jewish identity. Although the actual rituals of the seder differ only slightly among Jews from various origins, the ritual appurtenances vary greatly and tend to emulate the domestic objects of the local population.

Ritual objects produced for use during the Passover seder are characteristic of their contemporary historical art form. The group of three-tiered seder plates is a good example of such development, spanning the artistic styles from early nineteenth-century Neoclassicism through 1930s modernism to a contemporary art form. This evolution is further demonstrated by the Danzig piece, characteristic of local brass forms, and the Terezín example, demon-

Samaritans on Mount Gerezim after the slaughtering of the paschal lamb.

A Yemenite family at the seder table. Note the abundance of items on the seder plate.

A Bukharin family in traditional dress participating in the seder.
All photographs by David Harris, Jerusalem.

strating both the triumph of Judaism in the face of adversity and the impetus provided by *hiddur mitzvah*. A variety of materials was used to produce ceremonial objects for markets at different economic levels, including the fifteenth-century Spanish lusterware piece created for an affluent market and the simple pewter example dating from an era when pewter was a less costly alternative to silver.

Many artists have portrayed the Passover seder, capturing contemporary morés and modes of celebration. Bernard Picart depicted the sophistication of eighteenth-century Dutch Sefardic Jewry. Moritz Oppenheim's frequently copied image of the seder depicts the pleasures of Biedermeier domesticity, infused with the tension between assimilationist German nationalism and Jewish tradition. Participants in Oppenheim's seder wear stylish contemporary clothing, with the exception of a single figure in Eastern European or Hasidic dress, indicating the variety of Jewish experience in the mid nineteenth century. This image was so popular that it effectively served as a model of contemporary German Judaism. Copied in a variety of media, it was used to decorate many articles including the Herend seder dishes and etched glass goblet illustrated in this book.

Artists continue to visually explore the timelessness of the Passover story and to simultaneously imbue the seder with contemporary significance. Some artists, including Marc Chagall, El Lissitzky, and Ben Shahn, sought to create a modern Jewish art style by combining elements derived from traditional Jewish culture or folk art with a modern artistic vocabulary

and stylistic elements. The differences stemming from individual interest and idiosyncracies are apparent. In Lissitsky we see geometric forms stemming from cubism and Russian contructivism. Chagall uses the Exodus story as a component in the broader history of the Jewish people from ancient times until its most recent devastation during the Holocaust and the return to Jewish self-rule in the State of Israel. The haggadahs by Ben Shahn and Zeev Raban explore new calligraphic and figural forms. At the same time, Raban elected to incorporate a nationalistic element expressive of Zionism in his works. Reuven Rubin drew on the legacy of the Renaissance, translating it into modern idiom and using it to convey a contemporary message about the land of Israel and the Jewish people.

The universal themes of freedom celebrated at Passover and the injunction that each generation must regard themselves as having come out from Egypt continue to inspire contemporary artists to explore visual representation of the Passover story. Larry Rivers's three works, *The History of Matzah, the Story of the Jews* (1982–1984), incorporate elements of traditional and modern art. Other modern artists have maintained traditional formats, yet adapted them in innovative new ways. The seder set crafted of wood inlay by Lorelei and Alex Gruss uses the traditional three tiers, but includes a marquetry frieze of the Exodus depicting the many generations of Jewish experience, including a Holocaust survivor on the road to the Promised Land.

While the objects represent the meaning of Passover, they also add to its significance and suggest

Moritz Oppenheim. From *Passover Scenes from Old Jewish Family Life,*
Amsterdam, c. 1882. Collection of Belle Rosenbaum, Monsey, New York.

other perspectives from which the seder and the objects used for its celebration can be viewed through time. Most of these works were created in areas of cultural assimilation, and they speak to us of cross-cultural fertilization at a certain time and place— wherever Jews settled. Motifs and techniques borrowed from the local culture illustrate the power of fashion. Most of the pieces express the tension between two or more cultures since Jews were usually outsiders wherever they resided. Artwork created in Israel is infused with nationalist, Zionist spirit.

The seder is the reenactment of the Exodus experience. The haggadah instructs that "in each and every generation each man must regard himself as though he, himself, had come out from Egypt." The beautification of the seder table with family heirlooms and artifacts reflecting personal and contemporary esthetics defines the commemoration of the historical experience in the here and now.

Haggadah illustrations contribute to the sense that the Exodus from Egypt is not merely commemorated as an historical event, but as celebrated by the seder, it is part of the continuum of Jewish history. Haggadahs rarely portray the Exodus with accurate renditions of biblical costumes and landscapes, but rather use

contemporary models, so that in eighteenth-century manuscripts the Israelites look like central European courtiers. The Egyptian cities of Pithom and Ramses where the Israelites labored as slaves resemble Hamburg and Prague. The multisensory re-creation of the Exodus experience at the seder, a story that is told, shown, celebrated, and consumed, is intensified through the use of beautiful vessels, ceremonial objects, and illustrated haggadahs.

Bonni-Dara Michaels
Gabriel M. Goldstein

THE ART of PASSOVER

The Birds' Head Haggadah

C. 1300

Southern Germany

The classification of illuminated Hebrew manuscripts with figural decoration is broken down into regional groups: Sefardic, comprising North Africa, Spain proper, and the regions of France bordering on Spain, primarily Provence and Languedoc; Ashkenazic, mainly those areas which formed part of the empire of Charlemagne, including France and Germany; Oriental, encompassing the Islamic east (Egypt, Israel, Syria, Asia Minor, Iraq, and Iran); and Italian. The style of decoration is related most closely to other artworks, particularly illuminated manuscripts, of the region. For example, the decoration of a German Hebrew manuscript most closely resembles contemporary non-Jewish German manuscript decoration. The works which received decoration most often were Bibles, haggadahs, and prayer books; Torah scrolls were never decorated.

German haggadah manuscripts have illustrations of the biblical events narrated in the text, depictions of contemporary preparations for Passover, and text illustrations such as the four sons. Biblical illustrations are incorporated into the text rather than preceding or following it, as we find in Spanish versions, including the *Golden Haggadah*. Many male figures are depicted wearing a pointed hat which identified him as a Jew in thirteenth-century Germany and the Holy Roman Empire.

The Birds' Head Haggadah is so named because most of the human figures depicted in it have the heads of birds, although the use of bird heads is not consistent throughout the manuscript or even on individual pages. Approximately fifty Hebrew manuscripts are known which substitute bird or animal heads for human features.

The Birds' Head Haggadah was handed down in the Benedikt family during the nineteenth century. Until 1934 it was owned by Dr. Ludwig Marum of Karlsruhe who had married into the family; he died in Kisslau during the Holocaust.

Examination reveals that many of the images here have been cut, so that elements of landscape, the feet of various figures, and other aspects end abruptly. With use, the edges of pages in a manuscript, like those in any other well-read book, become torn and ragged. Illuminated manuscripts were cherished and precious; they were rarely discarded, despite signs of wear. To improve their appearance, the margins were often cut and the books rebound. Here, the heads of the figure in yellow and one of the figures of Moses (in red) have been trimmed.

This is the earliest surviving Ashkenazic illuminated haggadah. The text consists of verses from the hymn *Dayyeinu* ("It would have been enough for us."). This hymn enumerates the favors bestowed upon the Israelites by God, beginning with their departure from Egypt through the giving of the Torah to the building of the Temple in Jerusalem. *Dayyeinu* expresses thanks to God for his gifts, each of which would have been "enough." Several scenes from Exodus are shown. On the right, manna and quail fall from the sky. On the left, Moses receives the law and passes it on to the Jewish people.

Scribe: Menahem
Vellum, ink.
10 ⅝ × 7 ⅛ in. (27 × 18.5 cm).
The Israel Museum, Jerusalem. Ms. 180/57, fols. 22v–23.

וְלֹא שָׁקַע צָרֵינוּ
בְּתוֹכוֹ דַיֵּנוּ
אִלּוּ שָׁקַע צָרֵינוּ
בְּתוֹכוֹ
וְלֹא סִפֵּק צָרְכֵּינוּ בַּמִּדְבָּר
אַרְבָּעִים שָׁנָה דַיֵּנוּ
אִלּוּ סִפֵּק צָרְכֵּינוּ בַּמִּדְבָּר
אַרְבָּעִים שָׁנָה
וְלֹא הֶאֱכִילָנוּ
אֶת הַמָּן דַיֵּנוּ
אִלּוּ הֶאֱכִילָנוּ
אֶת הַמָּן

מִתַּן
תּוֹרָה

וְלֹא נָתַן לָנוּ
אֶת הַשַּׁבָּת דַיֵּנוּ
אִלּוּ נָתַן לָנוּ
אֶת הַשַּׁבָּת
וְלֹא קֵרְבָנוּ לִפְנֵי
הַר סִינַי דַיֵּנוּ
אִלּוּ קֵרְבָנוּ לִפְנֵי
הַר סִינַי
וְלֹא נָתַן לָנוּ
אֶת הַתּוֹרָה דַיֵּנוּ
אִלּוּ נָתַן לָנוּ
אֶת הַתּוֹרָה

Barcelona Haggadah

Mid 14th Century

Barcelona, Spain

Before 1492, Spain was divided into a number of principalities, one of which, Granada, was still under Moorish rule. This period in Spain had positive aspects for the Jews, both intellectual and social. The *Arba Turim*, a synthesis of Ashkenazic and Sefardic learning, was created by R. Yaakov ben Asher during the early years of the fourteenth century. At this time, Jewish courtiers still enjoyed a measure of favor, but persecution of the Jewish population was increasing. The Jews of Aragon were accused of spreading the Black Death and were massacred in 1348–9, and anti-Jewish preaching resulted in widespread forced conversions and massacres in 1391.

This manuscript includes the text of the haggadah, *piyyutim* (devotional poems), prayers, and readings for Passover. The upper initial-word panel (so called because it contains the first, or initial, word of the text) has several decorative elements. A man seated in a doorway points to the illustrations below him. He may represent Rashi, the acronym for Rabbi Shlomo ben Yitzhak (1040–1105), in whose writings we find an explanation for the naked figure astride a lion identified as Nebuchadnezzar, ruler of Babylon (605–562 B.C.E.), who conquered Jerusalem and sent its people into exile (597 B.C.E.). According to legend, Nebuchadnezzar had a pet lion with a snake curled around its neck. As punishment for overbearing pride and sinfulness, Nebuchadnezzar was stricken with madness. His advisors stripped him of his clothes and expelled him from the palace. As seen in this image, despite prohibitions against nudity in Jewish and Christian culture, nude figures are found here and elsewhere in both Christian and Jewish manuscripts.

The lower initial-word panel in this manuscript page contains the letters YKNHZ, a mnemonic for the order of the *kiddush* when a festival occurs on Saturday: one recites the blessing for wine (*Yayyin*), then the festival wine blessing (*Kiddush*), the candle blessing (*Ner*), and the separation between the Sabbath and the weekday (*Havdalah*), ending with the *she-hehiyanu* expressing thanks to God for enabling us to reach this time (*Zeman*). At the lower right, a man and youth recite the havdalah; the youth holds a twisted candle. An abbreviated hunt scene appears in the scrollwork at the upper right.

The other forms decorating the page are foliate scrolls and fantastic hybrids, known as drôleries, often found in medieval illuminated manuscripts.

Vellum, ink.
10 ⅞ × 7 ¼ in. (27.6 × 18.4 cm).
British Library, London. Add. Ms. 14761.

חל ל
להיות
במוצאי
שבת אומר
ויין
קדוש
נר
הבדלה זמן

Golden Haggadah

Early 14th Century
Barcelona, Spain

A Spanish scholar, Profiat Duran, wrote that books should be decorated and have fine calligraphy and bindings as such elements attract attention and are more pleasant to study, thus stimulating the mind. Beautiful, luxurious manuscripts such as the *Golden Haggadah,* a prime example of Duran's hypothesis, have invited study and delighted owners and readers for centuries.

The *Golden Haggadah* was probably produced in Barcelona around 1320. It contains a biblical picture cycle, the haggadah text, and *piyyutim* (devotional poems). The *Golden Haggadah* is one of a group of Spanish manuscripts in which the text of the haggadah is preceded by pages illustrating stories from the Bible. In this case, there are seventy-one narrative scenes illustrating Genesis 2:19 to Exodus 15:20. Many of these scenes have captions that appear to be contemporary with the haggadah text. This suggests that the captions contain elements derived from the *Midrash,* a body of lively and imaginative rabbinic interpretations of biblical writings.

Sometimes, additions to the text can tell us part of a manuscript's history. In this case, we learn that this haggadah manuscript was in Italy in the early seventeenth century, when a title page was painted noting that in 1602 the book was a gift from R. Joab Gallico of Asti to his daughter Rosa upon her marriage.

The Catholic Church has frequently required that offensive or "blasphemous" passages in Jewish texts be eliminated. Non-compliance resulted in the book being burned. In 1589 Pope Sixtus V (1520–90) banned any material contrary to Church teachings in Jewish books. An index of Hebrew books requiring alterations was established in 1595, listing passages to be deleted or revised. Sixtus appointed officials to revise the offensive books and provided them with a manual of rules. Censors would sign their work at the end of the manuscript. The *Golden Haggadah* was censored on three occasions: first by Fra Luigi da Bologna in 1599; next by Camillo Jaghel in 1613; and finally by Renato da Modena in 1626.

The illuminations reveal familiarity with examples of French Gothic style as filtered through contemporary Catalan works. The manuscript is known as the *Golden Haggadah* because of the burnished gold background in each scene. Evidence of French influence includes the gold background; ornamental hair curls; and the elegant swaying posture, small hands, and vivid gestures of the figures. While such influences may stem from manuscripts imported from France to Spain, it is also possible that the artist(s) trained in France or was perhaps a refugee from the 1306 expulsion of the Jews from France ordered by Philip IV the Fair (1268–1314). Many French refugees came to Barcelona at that time. Suggestions of perspective in the *Golden Haggadah* miniatures indicate familiarity with contemporary Italian works.

Vellum, ink, gold leaf.
9 ¾ × 7 ¾ in. (24.8 x 19.7 cm).
British Library, London. Add. Ms. 27210, fol. 10v.

Rylands Sefardic Haggadah

Mid to Late 14th Century
Catalonia

This manuscript was purchased in 1901 by the John Rylands Library at the University of Manchester, England, along with an extensive collection of Eastern and Western manuscripts acquired by the Earls of Crawford and Balcarres. At that time the library was two years old, having been opened in October 1899. Of the 6,000 manuscripts in this collection, 37 were written in Hebrew. This haggadah is known as the *Rylands Sefardic Haggadah* to distinguish it from several other haggadah manuscripts in the Rylands collection.

John Rylands (1801–88) was a merchant who amassed a large library at his home near Mansfield and provided funds for the printing of a Bible which he distributed without charge.

The Rylands haggadah contains a biblical picture cycle depicting episodes from the book of Exodus, from the story of Moses at the burning bush to the crossing of the Red Sea, ritual scenes, and text illustrations. The manuscript also contains the text of the haggadah, poems for Passover and for the Sabbath before Passover, and commentary on the haggadah. Most of the decoration was completed in the middle of the fourteenth century.

This panel consists of two horizontal compartments. Above each compartment is a quotation from Exodus identifying the scene below. These quotations are repeated in the right margin. In each scene, the figures are symmetrically arranged: the Jews on the left and the pharoah and his courtiers or counselors on the right. The setting is summarily indicated: a hillside with trees on which two figures, presumably Moses and Aaron, stand to demonstrate the havoc caused by the locusts (upper left); the throne upon which the pharoah sits, and an interior suggested by a wall and roof. The eye is prevented from going beyond the front plane of the picture by the scrollwork decorating the sky behind Moses and Aaron and by the elaborate cloth behind the Jews in the lower scene.

Stylistic elements suggest Italian influence. These include people's features and the modeling of their garments, rock and mountain formations, and the shape of the trees. The style of the *Rylands Sefardic Haggadah* also derives from contemporary Spanish, specifically Catalan, Gothic manuscript illustration. The closest parallel is a manuscript of the *Chronicles of the Aragonese King Jaime el Conquistador* dated 1343 produced under royal patronage for the court at Barcelona.

Italian influence on the Rylands manuscript probably stems from the trade connections between Catalonia and southern Italy, as Jews played a major role in these mercantile connections. The Jews of Catalonia, especially those of Barcelona, were a prosperous, scholarly community at this time. Their numbers were decimated by the Black Death of 1348. Later in the century, they were accused of desecration of the Host (c. 1367). In 1391, despite royal protection, the Jewish quarter was looted, many Jews were murdered, and others were given the choice between conversion and death.

Above: The plague of locusts. Below: The plague of darkness.
Vellum, ink.
11 3/16 × 9 3/16 in. (28 × 23 cm).
The John Rylands University Library, Manchester, England.
Heb. Ms. 6, fol. 17v.

ויעל הארבה על כל ארץ מצרים וינח בכל גבול מצרים ׃

ויהי חשך אפלה ולכל בני ישראל היה אור במושבותם

ויעל הארבה על
כל ארץ מצרים וינח
בכל גבול מצרים

ויהי חשך אפלה
ולכל בני ישראל
היה אור במושבותם

Darmstadt Haggadah

Late 15th Century
Germany

During the thirteenth century, a new form of Christian manuscript emerged. The *Little Office (or Hours) of Our Lady* became a separate book, no longer part of the Breviary, the liturgy used during services. These books were called Books of Hours and were intended for private worship. In addition to the *Little Office of Our Lady*, they might include penitential Psalms, the Litany, the office of the dead, the Suffrages (sufferings of the saints), texts from the Gospels, and a calendar noting special days of celebration. Books of Hours were ornamented with decorative borders, narrative scenes relating to the text, and elaborate initial letters. Many such books were produced by lay scribes and artists working for the aristocracy and for wealthy townspeople. They were often given as a gift to a bride on the occasion of her marriage.

It is interesting to note that the development of the separate haggadah manuscript, as opposed to those included in miscellanies, appears to date to the thirteenth century as did the development of the Book of Hours as a separate text.

The *Darmstadt Haggadah* has unusual decoration for an Ashkenazic haggadah manuscript. It lacks many common text and ritual illustrations and has no biblical scenes. A colophon gives the name of the scribe, Israel ben Meir from Heidelberg, but it is not certain that he was the illuminator as well.

The style represented by the miniature is known as International Gothic, as it prevailed across Europe. The text on this folio begins "Pour out thy wrath"; the first letter is separated from the rest of the word in an initial-letter panel. The decoration bears no relation to this text. Fashionably dressed men and women, apparently involved in discussion, are depicted in architectural settings. The pointed arches and vaulted ceilings are characteristic of Gothic architecture, and the clothing represents contemporary dress. Parallels for the modest necklines and covered heads of most figures, male and female, can be found in non-Jewish manuscripts. Only the hat of the figure at the right of the table in the lower scene is characteristically Jewish.

This scene portrays a group of men and women seated around a table. There are no kiddush cups or other elements pertaining to the seder, and the books of those at the table are closed. One might conclude that the Passover seder is over, and the guests are involved in continued discussion. However, since the round gold shapes are probably matzahs, one could assume that the seder is still in progress.

Vellum, ink.
14 × 9 ¾ in. (35.5 × 24.8 cm).
Darmstadt, Hessische Landes- und Hochschulbibliothek.
Cod. Or. 8, fol. 37v.

Hamburg Miscellany

Mid 15th Century
Germany, Middle Rhine

The *Hamburg Miscellany* contains prayers, *haftorot* (biblical selections from the prophets), the haggadah, *kinot* (memorial prayers for martyrs), *minhagim* (customs), and a calendar. The scribe was Isaac ben Simhah Gansmann who signed his name at the beginning of the calendar. Since the calendar begins with the year 1428, the manuscript was probably completed shortly before that time.

Among those commemorated by *kinot* are those martyrs who sacrificed themselves for *kiddush ha-Shem* (sanctification of the divine name), choosing death rather than conversion. The *kinot* refer to martyrs of Cologne, Würtzberg, Rothenburg, and Nuremberg and remind one of the frequent persecutions suffered by the Jews in fifteenth-century Germany. This diversity of locales makes it impossible to suggest a city of origin based on the *kinot*. Customs related in the *minhagim* section are those of Mainz, suggesting that the manuscript was completed and intended for use in or near that city.

The haggadah portion of the manuscript maintains the traditional form of Ashkenazic haggadah illustration, consisting of text illustrations, and biblical and ritual scenes. The scenes, some of which may be the work of Gansmann, are characteristic of contemporary German painting. The decoration includes initial-word and initial-letter panels as well as narrative scenes.

During this period, Jews were required to wear items of clothing that would identify them as Jews. The hat worn by the men in these scenes is a representation of the *Judenhut* (Jewish hat). The exact form of the hat varied with time. The shape differs slightly in *The Birds' Head Haggadah*. In the *Hamburg Miscellany* it is depicted in a variety of colors as well, here appearing in blue and white.

An unusual feature of this manuscript is the depiction of the Red Sea as actually being red in color. The rock formations of this scene, the depiction of recession, and the box-like interior of the scene above depicting Moses and Aaron before the pharaoh all demonstrate stylistic borrowings from contemporary Italian painting.

Vellum, ink.
11 ⅞ × 9 in. (30 × 22 cm).
Staats- und Universitätsbibliothek, Hamburg.
Cod. Heb. 37, fol. 29v.

כ מצרים מהראו
ויספרו
הברטשטיב אל פרעה ונכבד
אלוהם הוא ועל הם מהה
אז ויראו ישראל את המירהי
הגדלה אשר עשה
מג צים וייראו העם את יי ויאמינו ביי ובמשה
עבדו

Erna Michael Haggadah

c. 1400

Germany, Middle Rhine

Before the introduction of printing with movable type in the mid fifteenth century, books were written by hand and are referred to as manuscripts. The production of a manuscript was a long and complex process, more so when the text was to be decorated. Luxurious manuscripts were written on vellum although paper was available by the late Middle Ages. Manuscripts made of animal skins required special preparation. The animal hair had to be scraped and the skin treated so that both sides were suitable for writing. Sets of folded sheets were prepared. In some areas, the sheets were arranged so that when folded in codex (book) form, the sheets would be placed hair side facing hair side and skin side to skin side, presenting a uniform surface.

Next, the pages were ruled to make writing easier and more uniform. Measured pricks were made down the sides with a pointed instrument. These were joined by horizontal lines which could take the form of indentations made with a stylus or of lines made with lead.

The text was written with a reed or quill pen, using ink made from lampblack or iron salt. If a manuscript was to be decorated (illuminated), drawings were made. The word "miniatures" used to describe the pictures in manuscripts is derived from the use of minium (red lead) used in the preparation of the drawing. If gold leaf was to be used, it was applied next, and then colors were added.

Finally, the collection of sheets folded one within the other, called gathers or quires, would be sewn together and joined to a binding.

The earliest decorated Hebrew manuscripts to survive date from the ninth century. However, the repetition of certain motifs and the evidence of the wall paintings from the third-century Dura Europos Synagogue in Syria suggest a tradition of illuminated Hebrew manuscripts extending back to antiquity. Periodic bookburnings by Christian authorities, purposeful destruction of Jewish communities during wars and times of persecution, and accidental fires that ravaged the wooden structures of the Jewish ghettos make the survival of Hebrew illuminated manuscripts very surprising.

Most Ashkenazic haggadah manuscripts have marginal illustrations of textual, ritual, and biblical subjects. The *Erna Michael Haggadah,* however, has very few textual illustrations.

This is one of three scenes portraying figures seated at the Passover table. Although the scene occupies a full page, it is still referred to as a miniature. Within an elaborate architectural setting, we see four men seated at a table, their gestures indicating discussion. On the table are a large cup, a round matzah, a knife, and a book. Over their heads hangs a *judenstern,* an oil lamp used for the Sabbath and festivals.

The two men standing at either side of the table may be servants; one holds a vase, the other a container of some sort or perhaps another matzah. All the men are dressed in contemporary clothing, including the requisite pointed hat identifying them as Jews. Although there are four, not five, it is possible that they represent the rabbis at B'nai B'rak who became so engrossed in the commandment to elaborate upon the story of the Exodus that they failed to realize that dawn had arrived.

Parchment, ink, tempera, gold leaf.
13 ¾ × 10 ⅛ in. (36 × 25.5 cm).
The Israel Museum, Jerusalem. Ms.180/58, fol. 40.
Gift of Jakob Michael in memory of his wife, Erna Michael.

Ashkenazi Haggadah

Mid 15th Century
Cologne, Germany

Occasionally, a scribe or illuminator would record his name and the date on which he finished a manuscript in the colophon, an inscription at the end of a manuscript which can include the date and place the manuscript was produced as well as the name of the scribe and artist. It is here that we learn the name of the maker of this haggadah, "Feibusch, called Joel," and the man for whom the manuscript was made, Jacob Matthathias.

The Joel of the colophon has been identified as Joel ben Simeon, known as Feibusch the Ashkenazi from Cologne. The period of his artistic activity appears to stretch from 1449 to 1485. Five other haggadah manuscripts exist with his signature and in addition, he signed five illuminated Hebrew manuscripts of other texts bringing the total of his known works to eleven. He is described in other colophons as scribe, artist, or both and may have executed either text or images depending on his patron's commission. He is believed to have had his own workshop, comprising various individuals who laid out and ruled pages, copied the texts (haggadah, Bible, or prayer book), and painted the decorations.

The commentary in this manuscript is that of Rabbi Eleazar ben Judah of Worms (1169–c. 1230), a Kabbalist author of one of the most important treatises on Jewish law, *Sefer ha-Roke'ah*.

The text on this page begins "This is the bread of affliction . . ." It is interesting to note that, while many haggadah manuscripts depict both men and women seated around the seder table, here only men are seated under the hanging lamp (*judenstern*).

The *judenstern* is considered primarily a German ritual object. There are, however, some hanging lamps which were made and used in Italy.

Joel is believed to have come from Germany and either emigrated to Italy or visited there. The style of the figures and the perspectival placement of figures within the room all indicate the artist's familiarity with contemporary Italian painting.

The British Library in London has in its collection approximately seventy-five illuminated Hebrew manuscripts. These were gifts of non-Jews, including the first Earl of Oxford, Robert Harley (1661–1724), as well as Jews, among them Solomon da Costa Athias (1690–1769). He was the *gabbai,* the lay person responsible for the synagogue's rituals, honors, and charity collection and distribution, for London's Bevis Marks Synagogue and was descended from refugees from the Inquisition. A letter accompanying his donation states that the gift was a token presented in gratitude for the protection and freedom he enjoyed in England.

Vellum, ink, gold leaf.
14 ⅞ × 11 in. (37.5 × 28 cm).
The British Library, London.
Add. 14762, fol. 6a.

הא
לחמא עניא די אכלו אבהתנא
בארעא דמצרים כל דכפין
ייתי ויכל כל דצריך יתי
ויפסח השתא הכא לשנה
הבאה בארעא דישראל השתא

Rothschild Miscellany

1450–70

Ferrara, Italy

There have been Jews living in Italy since the time of the Maccabees in the second century B.C.E., and they have maintained a continuous presence through the medieval period down to the present. The growing prosperity of Italy from the fourteenth century was paralleled by Jewish prosperity, primarily derived from banking, which reached its height in the fifteenth century. Some level of intolerance did exist, however. In 1475 the old charge of ritual murder was raised against the Jews of Trent.

The artistic production of the Renaissance period in Italy is characterized by large-scale, monumental frescoes—Leonardo da Vinci's *Last Supper* and Michelangelo's Sistine Chapel ceiling—and by paintings on panels such as da Vinci's *Mona Lisa*. Yet, decorative handwritten manuscripts continued to be produced.

Scholars have dated the earliest surviving Hebrew illuminated manuscripts made in Italy to the thirteenth century. These were primarily Bibles, with decorated initial-word panels and some marginal decoration, but with no figural scenes. The number and type of Hebrew manuscripts with painted decoration increased throughout the fourteenth century, and human figures were included in the decorations. In these paintings, artists presented a wealth of detail on daily life and specific Jewish practices, in addition to depiction of biblical events and medical illustrations.

This manuscript is called a Miscellany because it contains a diverse group of religious texts from daily life and festivals, a group of secular texts and a collection of animal fables, the *Meshal ha-Kadmoni*. Among the religious texts is that of the haggadah. The *Rothschild Miscellany* contains over 300 images. Before it became part of The Israel Museum collection, it was part of the Rothschild collection in London.

The images here describe preparations preceding the commencement of Passover. A bearded man, the elder of the household, hunts for *hametz* with a feather, using a candle to illuminate dark corners of the cabinet in which he searches. The next two scenes show a woman mixing dough to make matzah, then rolling it; a young man pricks the dough with a pointed implement while another uses a long-handled, shovel-like tool known as a baker's peel to place the dough in an oven.

The artist demonstrates his awareness of contemporary manuscript illumination in the use of vanishing-point perspective and illusionistic decoration. The modeling of the figures manifests an awareness of human anatomy on the part of the artist. Classical, naturalistic style in Hebrew manuscripts commissioned by sophisticated Jewish patrons indicates their involvement in Italian Renaissance art and culture.

Vellum, ink, tempera, gold leaf.
8 ¼ × 6 ⅝ in. (21 × 16 cm).
The Israel Museum, Jerusalem. Ms. 18051, fol. 155v.
Gift of James R. de Rothschild, London.

הלכות חמץ ומצה
מהרמב"ם זצ"ל

זה ל סדר של פסח והגדה

קדש ורחץ כרפס יחץ מגיד ורחצה מוציא מצה מרור כורך שלחן עורך צפון ברך והלל נרצה

הלכות נטילה מפ"ו ימינך היו להראות נטילה החמץ מצה ומרור כורך דבר יהיה ידך

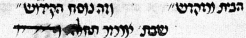

Passover Roundels

15th Century

Italy

Jews have resided in Italy as far back as the Roman period. During the fourteenth century, the indigenous Jewish community was joined by exiled Jews from Ashkenazic lands (Germany and parts of France). It was during the fifteenth century that the Jews of Italy truly flourished. Jews enjoyed the rewards of participation in Italy's prosperous banking network. Many Jews held professional positions such as physicians; still others were artisans, philosophers, or more traditional rabbinic scholars.

Fifteenth-century Italian illuminated manuscripts were usually richly decorated with ornate borders of naturalistic vegetal scrolls and frequently included illusionistic scenes such as those in the *Rothschild Miscellany*. Italian haggadahs, however, were usually simply decorated with a limited number of motifs, often depictions of specific rituals pertaining to the seder or of biblical events. Later fifteenth-century manuscripts such as the *Ashkenazi Haggadah,* demonstrate Ashkenazic iconographic influence by the themes and motifs used.

This manuscript consists of sixty-four round parchment leaves, eight across and eight down, joined together so that they can be folded to form a single circle. The text, written in Ashkenazic letters, includes the Passover haggadah, in the Italian tradition, and Psalms 113 and 114. The decoration consists of initial-word panels, a popular form of decoration of Italian manuscripts; the panels are alternately highlighted with red and black decorative frames consisting of flattened rather than illusionistic

foliate forms. For this reason, it is closer in form to thirteenth- and fourteenth-century Italian manuscripts, which were decorated using few colors, initial-word panels, simple painted motifs such as the matzah, and ornamental rather than figural marginalia.

The unusual shape of this haggadah manuscript may derive from a desire to evoke the form of the matzah, which was usually round during this period. This is one of three known extant manuscripts in this shape and demonstrates the creative versatility of the artisans who conceived and decorated Hebrew manuscripts.

This manuscript also includes decorative representations of matzah and *maror*. The rationale behind the use of a decorated initial or initial word, that it would act as a guide to indicate a division in the text, serves a dual purpose here. The image of the matzah signals a child or anyone who might not be able to read that this is the point in the seder where the purpose of the matzah is explained—to commemorate the haste with which the Israelites left Egypt.

Parchment, ink, paint, gold leaf.
Diameter (each roundel): 1 ½ in. (3.8 cm).
Hebrew Union College Skirball Museum, Los Angeles.
Gift of Mr. and Mrs. Felix Guggenheim.

Book of Exodus

1686

Iran

It is suggested that the existence of a Jewish community in Persia, now Iran, goes back to the time of exile after the destruction of the Temple by Nebuchadnezzar in 586 B.C.E. Some Jews who had established lives for themselves remained rather than returning to Palestine when permitted to do so under Cyrus (c. 538 B.C.E.). By the Hellenic period, there was a strong Jewish mercantile presence in Persia.

Important centers of Jewish learning were established at Sura and Pumbedita in Babylonia, part of the Persian empire from 539 B.C.E. until the empire was conquered by Alexander the Great in 331 B.C.E. The most important scholarly product of this region is the Babylonian Talmud, an interpretation of the *Mishnah,* a collection of oral law governing daily life taught in the academies.

The period from approximately 1597–8, when Shah Abbas I (1587–1629) established Isfahan as the capital of Persia, to its conquest in 1722 by the Afghans is considered a high point in Persian artistic history. Manuscript production flourished, especially under royal patronage. It was during this period that patronage also developed among merchants providing another market for art.

The earliest known inscriptions in Judeo-Persian, Persian written in Hebrew letters, date to the eighth century C.E. and vary according to the spoken dialect of different regions. In the fourteenth century the Jewish poet Shahin composed several works in Judeo-Persian, including the *Sefer Sharh Shahin al ha-Torah* based on biblical stories. This includes a book on Moses which is usually dated to c. 1327 C.E.

The majority of Persian paintings that have come down to use illustrate scenes of courtly life and love. However, a tradition of religious painting, illustrations of religious history or depictions of holy figures, existed in Persia. In the *Koran,* Muhammad ascends to heaven at night. There, he encounters the prophets who preceded him, including Moses. The ascension of Muhammad was sometimes depicted in manuscripts on his life, mystical writings, and in prefaces to poems praising God and Muhammad.

Muhammad and other prophets are often depicted in Persian art with a flame-shaped halo, like the halo of Moses in this picture, and commonly depicted wearing a veil that hides their features. This illumination of Moses presents another instance of the adaptation of local artistic vocabularly by the Jews. The pictorial space is entirely filled with figures or cloud forms. Clothing and wings are composed of dense areas of color, relieved by stylized folds in garments or the pattern of the wings.

Extant illuminated Judeo-Persian manuscripts all date to the seventeenth century. Their stylistic elements and the scenes they depict all parallel Persian manuscript painting. It is not known if there were Jewish painters working in Persian ateliers or whether a separate school of Jewish painters existed.

Paper, watercolor and gold powder, pen and ink.
11 × 6 ⅛ in. (28 × 15.5 cm).
The Israel Museum, Jerusalem.

נחת מרדן מוסי עה בא מלאיכה ניחת

תורי את

נכי גבת אית חוד בפאנס   שמארא שח אול בטנאתר
כה אינסת אנדידן אית גולתתה   אית גמטי גבור חק פרשגה

לאלא

בן ו

Prague Haggadah

1728–9

Moravia

I n the eighteenth century the art of the Hebrew illustrated manuscript flourished. This is particularly surprising since most manuscript production ceased after the invention of printing in the fifteenth century. Eighteenth-century Hebrew manuscripts were primarily commissioned by wealthy Jews, many of whom functioned as court officials. The *Hofjude* (Court Jew) represented the Jewish community before the ruler and often performed important financial functions such as raising revenues or collecting taxes.

Many factors encouraged *Hofjuden* to commission illustrated, handwritten copies of religious texts. Court Jews were sufficiently affluent to afford expensive manuscripts. They were exposed to the stylistic trends prevalent in the court and sought to emulate Christian collectors. Daughters of Court Jews frequently married important rabbinical scholars, and these families maintained a deep interest in traditional texts. Luxurious, illustrated manuscripts for personal use were frequently commissioned as gifts commemorating a marriage or other special events. Jews maintained scribal arts despite the invention of printing because of the need for Torah scrolls, *megillot, mezzuzot,* and *tefillin,* all of which must be handwritten by a scribe according to Jewish law.

The text and illustrations of this manuscript are largely based on the *Amsterdam Haggadah* printed in 1712, an indebtedness acknowledged on the frontispiece. The arrangement of the title page in this haggadah is modeled after similar compositions in contemporary printed books. The scribe was Nathan, son of Samson of Meseritsch.

This scene is a carefully rendered depiction of the young Moses slaying the Egyptian taskmaster and is almost identical to the copperplate rendition in the *Amsterdam Haggadah.*

The collection of The State Jewish Museum in Prague owes its existence to the Nazi confiscation of Jewish cultural treasures from throughout Bohemia and Moravia between 1942 to 1945. Jews of this region were deported to captivity and death, while their heirlooms were shipped to Prague to create a museum to an extinct race and a propaganda institute to justify the Final Solution. By the end of World War II, the Nazis had filled eight historic Jewish sites and more than fifty warehouses with over 140,000 artifacts attesting to the vibrancy of Jewish life in Bohemia and Moravia before the Holocaust.

Parchment, ink, gouache.
12 3/16 × 7 11/16 in. (31 × 19.5 cm).
The State Jewish Museum, Prague.
29 folios. Ms. 240.

מִן הָאָרֶץ · וַיְעַנּוּנוּ כְּמָה שֶׁנֶּאֱמַר לְמַעַן עַנּוֹתוֹ

בְּסִבְלֹתָם וַיִּבֶן עָרֵי מִסְכְּנוֹת לְפַרְעֹה אֶת **פִּתֹם**

וְאֶת **רַעַמְסֵס** · וַיִּתְּנוּ עָלֵינוּ עֲבֹדָה קָשָׁה כְּמָה

שֶׁנֶּאֱמַר וַיַּעֲבִדוּ מִצְרַיִם אֶת בְּנֵי יִשְׂרָאֵל בְּפָרֶךְ ·

וַנִּצְעַק אֶל יְיָ אֱלֹהֵי אֲבֹתֵינוּ וַיִּשְׁמַע יְיָ אֶת קֹלֵנוּ

וַיַּרְא אֶת עָנְיֵנוּ וְאֶת עֲמָלֵנוּ וְאֶת לַחֲצֵנוּ ·

וַנִּצְעַק אֶל יְיָ אֱלֹהֵי אֲבֹתֵינוּ · כְּמָה שֶׁנֶּאֱמַר

וַיְהִי בַיָּמִים הָרַבִּים הָהֵם וַיָּמָת

וַיִּבֶן אֶת פִּתֹם וְאֶת רַעַמְסֵס וַיִּפֶן כֹּה וָכֹה וַיַּרְא כִּי אֵין אִישׁ וַיַּךְ אֶת הַמִּצְרִי

Miniature Haggadah

1739

Central Europe

Miniature manuscripts and printed books were highly prized for their portability and as exquisitely detailed examples of the scribe or printer's skills.

The art of the hand-painted haggadah flourished during the eighteenth century, the heyday of the *Hofjude* (Court Jew.) A member of the prince's court in Germanic lands, the *Hofjude* advised the ruler in diplomatic and economic matters, commerce, and international trade. In return, the *Hofjude* received privileges and exemptions from restrictions normally applied to Jews. His position frequently enabled the *Hofjude* to be of service to his fellow Jews.

The *Hofjude* often acquired a high degree of cultural sophistication, emulating members of the prince's court. His privileged position allowed him to observe the latest fashions, and his affluence enabled him to commission elegant handwritten manuscripts rather than purchasing printed versions.

Eighteenth-century artists who illustrated haggadahs borrowed heavily from earlier, printed versions. Occasionally, they altered elements of preexisting images by updating costumes or added completely new scenes.

A Latin translation of the haggadah was issued in Frankfurt am Main, Germany, in 1512. The first printed haggadah translated into any language, it was published by a Christian to demonstrate that the haggadah contained no information offensive to the Church. Printed translations of the haggadah that did not incorporate the Hebrew text appeared as early as the seventeenth century with the *Venice Haggadah* of 1620 and the *Amsterdam Haggadah* of 1622, both of which were translated into Castilian Spanish. These were published for Marrano immigrants unfamiliar

with Hebrew so that they might be integrated into the Jewish community. Until the late eighteenth century, translations of the haggadah in Germany were in Yiddish rather than German. Yiddish translations accompanied the Hebrew text, as in the haggadah page illustrated here. One effect of the Enlightenment, which brought cultural assimilation to German Jews, was the decline of Hebrew literacy and the abandonment of Hebrew in favor of German texts.

The next to last song in the haggadah is *Ehad Mi Yodea* ("Who Knows One?"), a poem by an unknown author added to the Ashkenazic haggadah around the fifteenth century; it is not found in Yemenite or Sefardic haggadahs. This song and the last song, *Had Gadya* ("One Kid"), may have been added as an incentive to children to remain awake until the end of the seder. The song has thirteen verses, each of which received an illustration in many eighteenth-century haggadahs. The verses assign specific entities to each number; for example, three are the patriarchs Abraham, Isaac, and Jacob; five are the books of the Torah; ten are the commandments.

This illustration for *Ehad Mi Yodea* depicts twelve men, representing the twelve tribes of Israel. The old-fashioned garments suggest that the artist copied a preexisting image. Above the image is the text in Hebrew; below, the text is repeated in Yiddish.

Vellum, ink.
4 × 3 in. (10.5 × 8.5 cm).
Library of the Jewish Theological Seminary, New York.

שְׁנֵים עָשָׂר מִי יוֹדֵעַ · שְׁנֵים
עָשָׂר אֲנִי יוֹדֵעַ ·
שְׁנֵים עָשָׂר שִׁבְטַיָּא · אַחַד עָשָׂר כּוֹכְבַיָּ'
עֲשָׂרָה דִבְּרַיָּא · תִּשְׁעָה יַרְחֵי לֵידָה · שְׁ
שְׁמוֹנָה יְמֵי מִילָה · שִׁבְעָה יְמֵי שַׁבַּתָּא שִׁשָּׁה
סִדְרֵי מִשְׁנָה · חֲמִשָּׁה חוּמְשֵׁי תוֹרָה ·

צוועלף מול' דוש מיז מבר וער · מול' דמט ·עלבין וויט
מיך · לוועלן זינד ימ גטוועבט · מיול ·זין דימ ט
טטערין · לעהין זין דימ לעהין גיבמט · כיין זין דימ גוויכונג
מכט זין דימ בטכיידונג · זיבן זין דימ פ̇יורוונג · זעקט ·
זין דימ לערונג · פ̇ינן זין דימ ביכ̇ר פ̇יר זין דימ איטר כו'

Raban Haggadah

1925
Israel

The son of a merchant, Zeev Raban (Rabitzky)(1890–1970) was born in Poland and received a traditional Jewish as well as a secular education. He first studied art in his home town of Lodz. Subsequently, he attended the Kunstgewerbeschule in Munich, the Ecole des Beaux Arts, Paris, and the Royal Academy in Belgium. Returning to Paris, he met Boris Schatz, founder of the Bezalel school of arts and crafts in Israel. Schatz hired Raban to teach sculpture and anatomy there. In 1914 Raban became director of the repoussé department and began to develop his own unique style.

By the late 1920s, Raban was active in the Graphic Press at Bezalel along with Meir Gur-Arieh, and together they founded the Industrial Art Studio. After the 1929 closing of the Bezalel school, Raban supported himself and his family by producing works on commission. In 1949 Raban was commissioned to design tombstones for soldiers of the Haganah, the underground Jewish defense organization of Israel founded in 1920.

During his formative years as an artist, Raban was exposed to various forms of German *Jugendstil* and French Art Nouveau with its sinuous curves and focus on the female as subject. The passion for idealized Orientalism remained prevalent from the nineteenth century. Subject matter, color scheme, and decorative patterns were borrowed from exotic lands.

By the 1920s Zionism was a world movement dedicated to the preservation of Jewish tradition and of Judaism, the revival of Hebrew as a daily language, and the settlement of Jews in Israel, their traditional home. Boris Schatz was inspired by Zionism to create a "Jewish Style," choosing Jewish subjects and combining realistic elements with stylized plants and animals of Israel, Jewish symbols, adaptations of archaeological motifs, and the serpentine line and elongated figure of Art Nouveau.

Raban adapted these elements to create his own personal style. In his works we often see idealized biblical landscapes lush as a garden in a Persian miniature. His landscape is never topographic in a realistic sense; it is idealistic, calm, and timeless.

Raban's placement of the figures of the Israelites leaving Egypt in a frieze, placed at the foreground of the composition on the top of the page, is stylistically similar to ancient Egyptian and Assyrian paintings and relief sculpture. The angel wrestling with Jacob at left is modeled after Assyrian reliefs, although the recession of the figures in the background is from Western tradition. The angels in the depiction of Jacob's dream are also derived from representations of Assyrian winged deities.

There is a suggestion of sociopolitical meaning in Raban's works; he was after all, a member of a group with a specific political agenda. The land of Israel he represents in the haggadah has a dual nature. It is both a presentation of biblical events and an arena in which events were being shaped at the time.

Watercolor and pen and colored ink on paper; text inserts on parchment.
9 ⅞ × 13 ¾ in. (25 × 35 cm).
Collection of the Schlesinger Family, Tel Aviv.

וַיֵּרֶד מִצְרַיְמָה אָנוּס עַל פִּי הַדִּבּוּר.

וַיָּגָר שָׁם מְלַמֵּד שֶׁלֹּא יָרַד יַעֲקֹב אָבִינוּ לְהִשְׁתַּקֵּעַ בְּמִצְרַיִם אֶלָּא לָגוּר שָׁם שֶׁנֶּאֱמַר וַיֹּאמְרוּ אֶל פַּרְעֹה לָגוּר בָּאָרֶץ בָּאנוּ כִּי אֵין מִרְעֶה לַצֹּאן אֲשֶׁר לַעֲבָדֶיךָ כִּי כָבֵד הָרָעָב בְּאֶרֶץ כְּנָעַן וְעַתָּה יֵשְׁבוּ נָא עֲבָדֶיךָ בְּאֶרֶץ גֹּשֶׁן.

בִּמְתֵי מְעָט כְּמָה שֶׁנֶּאֱמַר בְּשִׁבְעִים נֶפֶשׁ יָרְדוּ אֲבֹתֶיךָ מִצְרַיְמָה וְעַתָּה שָׂמְךָ יְיָ אֱלֹהֶיךָ כְּכוֹכְבֵי הַשָּׁמַיִם לָרֹב.

וַיְהִי שָׁם לְגוֹי מְלַמֵּד שֶׁהָיוּ יִשְׂרָאֵל מְצֻיָּנִים שָׁם גָּדוֹל וְעָצוּם כְּמָה שֶׁנֶּאֱמַר וּבְנֵי יִשְׂרָאֵל פָּרוּ וַיִּשְׁרְצוּ וַיִּרְבּוּ וַיַּעַצְמוּ בִּמְאֹד מְאֹד וַתִּמָּלֵא הָאָרֶץ אֹתָם.

רָב כְּמָה שֶׁנֶּאֱמַר רְבָבָה כְּצֶמַח הַשָּׂדֶה נְתַתִּיךְ וַתִּרְבִּי וַתִּגְדְּלִי וַתָּבֹאִי בַּעֲדִי עֲדָיִים שָׁדַיִם נָכֹנוּ וּשְׂעָרֵךְ צִמֵּחַ וְאַתְּ עֵרֹם וְעֶרְיָה.

Ben Shahn Haggadah

1931

United States

Ben Shahn (1898–1969) was born in Kovno, Lithuania and came to the United States with his family when he was eight. He worked as an apprentice in lithography and studied at the Educational Alliance, the National Academy of Design, and the Art Students League in New York. After traveling to North Africa and Europe, Shahn setttled in Brooklyn, New York.

Kovno was a center of socialism, and Shahn became involved in social issues revolving around discrimination. He produced a series of works relating to the infamous Dreyfus trial of 1894, depicting various people connected with it. In the 1930s, Shahn painted a series of pictures to protest the trials and subsequent execution of Nicola Sacco and Bartolomeo Vanzetti in 1927.

The period after the first World War saw a return to the use of recognizable figural imagery in art. However, abstraction and collage had released the artist from the traditional need to arrange figures in sequential narrative.

In Shahn's *Haggadah* we see elements associated with the traditional story of Passover juxtaposed for maximum visual impact rather than being laid out in obvious visual sequence. Among the elements of the story seen in this image are the slaying of the firstborn of the Egyptians, last of the ten plagues, and Moses, staff upraised, confronting the serpent of the pharaoh's magicians.

Other contemporary elements of Shahn's style include the use of flat areas of color, decorative patterning, and shallow space. The haggadah illustrates a fight against oppression which occurred in the past. Yet each generation is called upon in the haggadah to view the release from Egypt as if it happened in its own time. By illustrating the haggadah in a contemporary style, Shahn expressed his interest in social issues and his Jewish identity through the medium of current artistic vocabulary.

This is one of the earliest works by Shahn which has both a Jewish theme and incorporates calligraphy. Later, he was to produce many fine works joining both in his personal, innovative style, including his version of a *ketubbah* (a Jewish marriage contract) and a book on the Hebrew alphabet called *The Alphabet of Creation*.

Printed haggadah.
15 ⅜ × 11 ⅝ in. (39 × 4.45 cm).
Courtesy of Mrs. Ben Shahn.

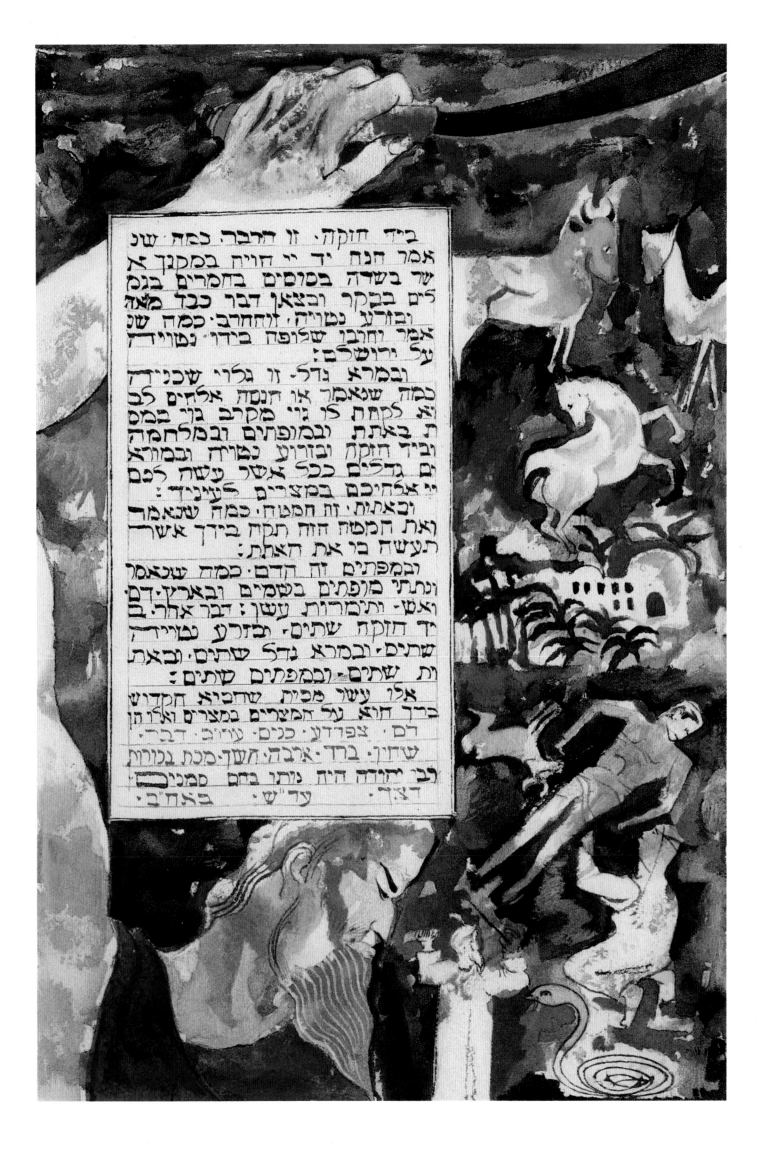

ביד חזקה · זו הדבר · כמה שנ
אמר הנה יד יי חויה במקנך א
שר בשדה בסוסים בחמרים בגמ
לים בבקר ובצאן דבר כבד מאד
ובזרע נטויה · זו החרב · כמה שנ
אמר יחרבו שלופה בידו נטויה
על ירושלם ·
ובמרא גדל · זו גלוי שכינה
כמה שנאמר או הנסה אלהים לב
וא לקחת לו גוי מקרב גוי במס
ת באתת ובמופתים ובמלחמה
וביד חזקה ובזרוע נטויה ובמורא
ים גדלים ככל אשר עשה לכם
יי אלהיכם במצרים לעיניך ·
וכאתיי · זה המטה · כמה שנאמר
ואת המטה הזה תקח בידך אשר
תעשה בו את האתת ·
ובמפתים זה הדם · כמה שנאמר
ונתתי מופתים בשמים ובארץ דם
ואש · ותימרות עשן : דבר אהר · ב
יד חזקה שתים · וזרע נטויה ·
שתים · ובמרא גדל שתים · ובאת
ת שתים · ובמפתים שתים :
אלו עשר מכות שהביא הקדוש
ברך הוא · על המצרים במצרים ואלו הן
דם · צפרדע · כנים · ערוב · דבר ·
שחין · ברד · ארבה · חשך · מכת בכורות
רבי יהודה היה נותן בהם סמנים ·
דצ"ך · עד"ש · באח"ב :

Passover Banner

1828–9
Alsace (?)

Wherever they lived, Jews adopted customs from the general population and adapted regional esthetics and culture to create a distinct local Jewish identity. Although the actual rituals of the seder differ only slightly among Jews from various origins, the ritual appurtenances used on seder nights vary greatly and tend to emulate the domestic objects of the local population.

The first evidence of Jews in Alsace, France's smallest and easternmost province, is found in the writings of Benjamin of Tudela, the well-known medieval traveler and chronicler, who reported on the Jews of Strasbourg in the twelfth century. In 1349 Jews were accused of spreading the Black Death and were expelled from the towns of Alsace. Unable to settle in towns and cities, Jews settled in the villages of the region. At the time of the French Revolution in 1789, more than half of French Jewry lived in Alsace. Alsatian Jewry lived in almost 200 villages across the province's agricultural plain and absorbed many local village traditions, adapting local dress, cuisine, language, manners, and folklore into their religious and daily lives. Alsatian Jews were emancipated following the French Revolution, but even after the proclamation of the equality of Jews in 1791, changes in status were fiercely opposed by segments of the local population and were only slowly adopted.

This banner is an example of the melding of Jewish ritual practice with Alsatian village custom. In Alsatian homes, an embroidered show towel was hung near the front door and was used to cover and hide soiled towels used for handwashing. Alsatian Jews adapted this custom and created elaborately decorated seder show towels used for the handwashing ceremonies preceding the eating of the *karpas* (green vegetable) and matzah at the seder. These painted or embroidered seder show towels, known as *Sederzwëhl* in Judeo-Alsatian, were used to cover utilitarian towels with which the hands were dried on the seder night.

The banner was probably used as a seder show towel and is decorated with a large central bouquet, a typical Alsatian motif found on Jewish, Christian, and secular artifacts. This bouquet may be modeled on similar arrangements of paper flowers, an Alsatian craft specialty and popular cottage industry of the region. Alsatian Jews used paper flowers to create Torah crowns, another adaptation of local folk art customs for Jewish religious practice.

Linen, painted; open weave, knotted cotton fringe.
55 ½ × 16 ⅓ in. (141 × 41.5 cm).
The Jewish Museum, New York.
Gift of Dr. Harry G. Friedman.

Ceremonial Towel

c. 1800

Europe, Western Ashkenazic

This robustly embroidered towel was used for the ritual washing of hands preceding the eating of the *karpas* dipped in salt water and before eating matzah at the seder. The towel bears a Hebrew inscription indicating the name of the probable owner of this towel: "Avraham Heller."

The towel is part of a matched set of seder textiles, consisting of a pillowcase and towel. Participants at the Passover seder recline against pillows as a symbol of their freedom and prosperity, a practice based on the classical Greek model. The entire seder structure is reminiscent of the format of the classical Greek symposium during which food and wine stimulated discussion and analysis of topics of interest.

The decoration of this towel is characteristic of late eighteenth- and nineteenth-century central European folk embroidery. Red thread embroideries on a neutral ground were frequently produced in this region.

The rampant animals embroidered on this towel may be mere decorative devices, as animal motifs are frequently found on folk textiles. However, lions are very often found on ceremonial textiles and metalwork. The arrangement of two flanking lions is similar to compositions frequently found on European ark curtains and Torah shields. The lion, symbol of Judah, is often used to invoke majesty. The crowns atop the heads of the lions accentuate the majestic nature of these animals. A lion with two tails indicates superior strength and is the symbol of both Bohemia and Prague, suggesting that this towel may have originated in this region. The rampant posture of the lions and stags and the decorative bands of pattern on the animals' midsections suggest that the embroiderer may have been influenced by similar representations found on heraldic devices.

The embroiderer has used a variety of inventive chevron and checked patterns throughout, imbuing the decorative floral and animal motifs with playful energy. The direction of the filling stitches on the lions' bodies varies, creating a texture suggesting fur, adding to the ferocity of these animals. The geometric patterns filling the Hebrew characters and the overall forms of the characters, adorned with circular motifs and ornamental ascenders, as in the Hebrew letter *lamed*, are reminiscent of the decoration of Hebrew lettering found in medieval Ashkenazic manuscripts. Similarly decorated Hebrew inscriptions are found on central European embroidered Torah binders dating from the eighteenth century on.

The combination of lions with deer found on this towel may be inspired by the instruction in *Ethics of the Fathers* 5:23: "Be . . . fleet as the hart and mighty as the lion to do the will of your Father who is in Heaven."

Undyed linen embroidered with red cotton and polychrome silk; border of knitted undyed linen lace.
72 ⅞ × 18 ⁵⁄₁₆ in. (185 × 46.5 cm).
The Jewish Museum, New York.
Gift of Mrs. E.S. Fechimer, 1941.

Seder Towel

1821

Alsace, France/Southern Germany

Hands are ritually washed twice during the seder service—prior to the eating of the *karpas* and again prior to the blessings recited over the matzah.

The first washing recalls the purity laws in effect during the time of the Temple in Jerusalem. It was believed that dry food was not susceptible to becoming impure. Since one could be carrying a form of impurity transmitted by the hands, ritual purification was required before coming in contact with moist food. Once the Temple was destroyed, the system of purity and impurity disappeared. The ritual washing is done today primarily as a reminder of the ancient laws. A similar recollection of the Temple service at the Passover seder is the roasted shankbone, symbolizing the paschal lamb.

The second washing of the hands is preceded by a blessing since traditional Jewish law required ritual washing of the hands before eating a formal meal, defined as one at which bread, either leavened or unleavened, is eaten. The ritual washing of the hands also serves as a reminder that the table on which one eats is akin to the altar of the Lord in the Temple in Jerusalem. Eating is therefore a holy activity, one that should be approached in purity.

The Passover towel shown here was made in Alsace, France, in 1821. This was a time of great change for the Jewish community in Alsace. The French ruled the area and emancipated the Jews. Following the emancipation of French Jewry, certain laws that were disadvantageous to all French Jews were passed but were enforced primarily in the Alsatian area.

The cartouche near the top records the year the towel was made according to traditional Jewish chronology, [5]581, which corresponds to 1821. Below this is the name "Abraham Blümche" flanked by two columns spanned by an arcade from which hangs a lit candelabrum. Featured prominently below the name is a man smoking a pipe, leading a goat by a rope past a beautifully detailed oak leaf bearing acorns. It is possible that this image is a reference to the song *Had Gadya,* but it may also be a depiction of Blümche himself.

This seder show towel, known in Judeo-Alsatian as *Sederzwëhl,* demonstrates the blending of Jewish ritual practice with Alsatian folk custom. It was customary in Alsatian homes to hang an embroidered show towel to cover and hide soiled towels. Alsatian Jews adapted this custom and created elaborate show towels for seder hand-washing ceremonies.

The large central floral arrangement located in the lower portion of this towel is a typical Alsatian motif. The vase is decorated with the blue, white, and red tricolor indicating the owner's French patriotism. This assertion of French identity is of particular interest when viewed in the context of the ongoing Franco-German tensions in Alsace-Lorraine at the time.

Undyed linen embroidered with polychrome silk threads; silk ribbon trim.
50 × 15 ½ in. (127.1 × 39.6 cm).
Hebrew Union College Skirball Museum, Los Angeles.

Embroidered Matzah Bags

1890–1, Romania

19th Century, Poland/Hungary/Eastern Europe

These two matzah bags represent the inventive diversity of material and ornamentation used for embroidered textiles of identical form and function. The circular decoration on both matzah bags echoes the shape of the bag itself, made to hold the special round, handmade matzah placed within. Each has three compartments to separate the matzahs, and a tab jutting out from the circle identifies the matzahs which represent the three groups of Jewish people, *Kohen* (the Priests), *Levi* (Levites), and *Yisrael* (Israelites). Both make use of wreath-like floral motifs to encircle text referring to the Passover seder. Here the similarity ends.

The yellow matzah bag is decorated with roses and embroidered text. The outer inscription lists the order of the Passover seder in a poem form some authorities attribute to Rashi, Rabbi Solomon ben Isaac (1040–1105). It is intended to provide the participant with a sense of awe at the miracles associated with the Exodus from Egypt.

The fifteen stages of the seder outlined here remind one of the fifteen steps the Levites climbed to reach the holy Temple. Embroidered in the center of this matzah bag is the phrase *Le-Shanah ha-baah be-Yerushalayim*—"Next year in Jerusalem."

The crown on the green matzah bag could be an allusion to one of the three crowns mentioned in *Ethics of the Fathers*—Torah, priesthood, and royalty—or to the crown of a good name. The sheep refer to the Passover sacrifices at the time of the Temple. The fish may be connected with the legend that a feast including the Leviathan, a huge, whale-like fish, would usher in the messianic era. The scales and fins, denoting a kosher fish, are cleverly elaborated with sequins.

The dedicatory inscription embroidered in the center of the green matzah bag indicates that it was presented to Natan Moses as a gift from a school in Jerusalem. Ceremonial objects, often made of materials associated with the Holy Land such as olive wood or stone, were frequently presented to patrons of Jerusalem-based institutions. Passover was frequently an occasion for fund-raising efforts. Traditionally, *Maot Hittin,* funds for wheat, were collected to provide matzahs for the needy.

Above: Undyed silk/cotton satin, embroidered with polychrome silk.
Diameter: 14 9/16 in. (37 cm).
The Jewish Museum, New York.
Gift of Mrs. Sol Chesler in memory of her parents, Israel Selig and Feige Adelman, 1960.

Below: Velvet; silk and metallic embroidery; appliqué fish scales.
Diameter: 24 in. (61 cm).
Hebrew Union College Skirball Museum, Los Angeles.

Matzah Bag

19th Century
Germany

Flowers have long formed part of the decorative vocabulary of the embroiderer. The delicate and intricate design of this matzah bag reflects this as well as demonstrating the skill of the needle-woman whose initials "S.N." appear in the center. The Hebrew inscription in the center identifies the special purpose of this matzah bag—"Y[ou shall observe] the Feast of Unleavened Bread."

Sewing was a practical skill, and girls were taught while young to mend clothing and to use more decorative stitching for such items as a bridal trousseau or home furnishings.

The creation of decorative needlework signified the social position of the family. The more affluent women were at leisure to produce decorative objects for the table and for festivals. For a Jewish woman there was also the tradition of *hiddur mitzvah*, the beautification of items used for ritual observances. For Passover, she could embroider a matzah bag such as this, a pillow for her husband to recline upon during the seder, and a towel for use after the ritual hand-washing. Other needle work was presented to the synagogue: Torah mantles and binders, ark curtains, and readers' desk covers.

Embroidered textiles were produced by women based on skills and patterns learned in the home and were made to be used, not sold. By the nineteenth century, pattern books were fairly common and provided examples of the latest styles in contemporary needlework. However, rather than designing her own pattern, the embroiderer had many other options. Pieces could be purchased with a printed design that had only to be stitched over; an artist could be commissioned to draw a pattern; or a paper pattern could be purchased, traced or sewn over, and then removed.

Attractive engravings or patterns could be copied by pouncing. Holes were pierced around the outline of the picture selected and filled with powder or charcoal, often kept in a special container called a pounce box. The outline produced was then filled in with stitchery.

What differentiates Jewish ceremonial needlework is its use and when present, the inscriptions, rather than the decorative techniques or the materials.

Undyed silk/cotton satin, embroidered with polychrome silk.
15 ⅛ × 16 in. (38.5 × 40.5 cm).
The Jewish Museum, New York.
Gift of Mr. and Mrs. Max Gottschalk.

Afikomen Pouch

19th Century
China

T he Babylonian Talmud teaches that everyday items may be used for religious ceremonies, but ceremonial objects may not be debased by use for secular purpose. Throughout the ages, Jews have adapted various splendid decorative objects to beautify the celebration of religious practice. A wide variety of materials has been transformed from secular to sacred use. Bridal dresses have often been transformed into luxurious Torah ark curtains. Brass plaques from soldiers' helmets were made into back-plates for Hanukkah lamps. During the eighteenth and nineteenth centuries, silver boxes made for the storage of sugar were frequently adapted to hold the *etrog* (citron) for the festival of Sukkot.

This matzah bag, crafted of Chinese embroidery, was probably adapted for use as an *afikomen* container to beautify the seder ritual. The fabric predates its use as a Jewish ceremonial object.

Archaeological finds attest to the antiquity of the tradition of fine embroidery in China which reaches as far back as the second century B.C.E. While princesses and wealthy women practiced fine embroidery as a pastime, both men and women were professional embroiderers. They produced decorative wall and bed hangings, articles of clothing, purses, shoes, spectacle cases, and other items. Chinese embroidered silk was a luxury commodity imported to Europe by the East India Company during the seventeenth century, and later, fashionable Europeans sent silks and satins to China to be skillfully and inexpensively embroidered.

There is no evidence to suggest whether this bag was used ceremonially in China or if it was adapted for use in Europe from a piece of Chinese embroidery. It is interesting to note, however, that a Jewish community of approximately 1,000 existed in Kaifeng in central China from the eleventh century A.D. until the death of its last rabbi in 1800. After that, the Jews of Kaifeng dispersed or were assimilated into the Chinese culture.

The characteristic Chinese floral motifs on this bag are composed of stitches similar to those popular in European embroidery: the seed stitch or French knot, satin and chain stitches, and couching. Using vibrant tones of blue and gold and a masterful blending of stitches, the embroiderer has created a piece of art—one with texture, shading, and great beauty.

Cotton, satin, embroidered with silk and metallic thread.
Diameter: 5 ¾ in. (14.6 cm).
Hebrew Union College Skirball Museum, Los Angeles.

Embroidered Matzah Bags

1896, Romania

1903–4, Moravia

Early in the nineteenth century, colored needlework patterns were introduced, making stitchery patterns easier to copy. The earliest publications of needlepoint patterns copying famous paintings, floral borders, and bouquets were produced in Berlin. When the fashion spread across Europe and to England, such patterns were referred to as Berlin patterns. They were reproduced in popular ladies' magazine, books about stitchery, and even dictionaries of needlework categorizing types and stitches of many nations. An up-to-date choice could be made, possibly from patterns suggested for the borders of the immensely popular, traditional Victorian mottoes such as "Home Sweet Home," and combined with texts suitable for use at the Passover seder.

The creation of decorative fabric covers for the three matzahs on the seder table has a long history. The blessing recited on eating matzah is frequently a decorative element on such textiles. In the past, it was embroidered by hand in silk and wool on silk or canvas backgrounds.

The skill of the needlewoman, her choice of decorative pattern, the intricacy of the pattern, the colors she used, all determined the appeal of the piece. They also conveyed a wealth of information to her contemporaries regarding her upbringing, her station in life, her level of taste, and her character.

The matzah bag on the left was embroidered by Pauline Rosenberg in 1896 on a square meshed cotton canvas called either Penelope or Berlin canvas. Working a pattern on this canvas was much simpler than conventional embroidery on fabric since the squares were comparatively large and the stitchery less complicated.

The first blessing recited over matzah during the Passover seder is the *ha-Motzi,* the blessing recited throughout the year before eating any form of leavened or unleavened bread: "Blessed art Thou, Lord our God, King of the Universe, who brings forth bread from the earth." Pauline Rosenberg embroidered her matzah cover with the second of the blessings recited over the matzah, a blessing recited only during the seder: "Blessed art Thou, Lord our God, King of the Universe, who has sanctified us by His commandments and commanded us to eat matzah."

The decoration on the velvet matzah bag consists of inscriptions listing the order of the Passover seder, the names of the foods placed on the seder plate, the year in which the piece was made, the name of the man for whom it was made, and decorative motifs including a wine goblet.

Many Ashkenazi communities used matzah bags divided into three sections with inscribed tabs. The three matzahs distinguish Passover from the Sabbath and other festivals on which only two loaves are required and commemorate the three matzahs required as an offering of thanks in the days of the Temple from people who were freed from prison, recovered from an illness, or crossed a desert (Leviticus 7:12). Since the Israelites leaving Egypt fit all three categories, a thanks-offering of three matzahs is made.

Left: Cotton canvas, embroidered with wool.
14 × 14 in. (35.5 × 35.5 cm).
The Jewish Museum, New York.
Gift of Fanny Goldberg, 1960.

Right: Velvet embroidered with cotton, cotton and metallic fringe, cotton cord, linen damask lining.
17 ½ × 12 7/16 in. (44.5 × 31.5 cm).
Provenance: Jewish Museum, Mikulov (Nikolsburg), Moravia. The State Jewish Museum, Prague.

Lusterware Passover Plate

c. 1480

Spain

Jews probably first settled in Spain under the Roman Empire. Under Visigothic rule (412–711 C.E.), Jews were frequently persecuted. In 613 King Sisebut decreed that Jews must convert to Christianity or leave the country. The Muslim conquest of Spain in 711 ushered in an era of coexistence between Muslim, Christian, and Jew. The Golden Age of Jewish Spain in the eleventh and twelfth centuries saw the fruition of this cultural melding, with Jews active in science, philosophy, poetry, and statesmanship. However, Jewish life in Spain was never completely idyllic; there was an ever-present undercurrent of anti-Semitic feeling and overt acts of violence against Jews.

Lusterware is an expensive, sumptuous pottery, believed to have originated in Egypt in the eighth century C.E. The production of lusterware involves two firing processes. First, glazed pottery is fired at a high temperature; then the piece is painted above the glaze with metallic oxides of silver and copper and fired again at a lower temperature. This second firing produces the iridescent metallic sheen.

Inscriptions on ceramics were a component of the Islamic heritage of Spanish lusterware. The use of decorative calligraphic inscriptions is a trademark of Islamic art. Spanish lusterware plates made for Christian patrons with Latin inscriptions are also known. The existence of similarly decorated ceramics for Muslims, Christians, and Jews from medieval Spain is an indication of the cultural interplay between the various religions of this society.

This plate is inscribed with the Hebrew words for "Passover, matzah, bitter herbs, seder" and contains numerous spelling errors. This may indicate that the painter was unfamiliar with Hebrew. However, textual errors are frequently found in Jewish manuscripts and artifacts.

Illustrations in contemporary Spanish illuminated manuscript haggadahs give us insights into the possible use of this plate. There are no similar plates depicted on seder tables. Matzahs were distributed to the community at the synagogue, and a manuscript in the British Museum shows the matzahs stacked for distribution on a similar plate. The size and shape of this plate suggest that it was used for communal matzah distribution.

Earthenware, tin-enameled.
Diameter: 22 ½ in. (57 cm).
The Israel Museum, Jerusalem.

Pewter Passover Plate

19th–20th Century

Central Europe (?)

Until the middle of the nineteenth century, the Jewish quarter of Prague was a densely populated area of narrow, dark streets. In the 1890s the streets were widened, and buildings were demolished, with the exception of a few such as the Altneuschul, considered to be landmarks. A Jewish quarter had existed in Prague since the ninth or tenth century. Until the sixteenth century, Jews living in the area were not forced to live in an enclosed space, as they were in other cities, but could reside where they wished and move with a certain amount of freedom. Most Jews chose to reside near their religious structures—synagogue, ritual bath, and schools.

In the aftermath of the revolutions of 1848–9, Jews were legally granted the rights, freedoms, and privileges of their non-Jewish neighbors. Yet, the nationalism expressed subsequently manifested a certain amount of confusion. While some Jews were loyal to the German/Habsburg house, others joined the Bohemian/Czech cultural and linguistic revival.

The seder plate shown here is made of pewter, an alloy primarily composed of tin. Tin is brittle and is therefore mixed with brass, lead, copper, and other alloys to produce a harder end product. Due to the toxicity of lead, stringent rules governed the amount and quality of the lead used to produce pewter. Items made of pewter are usually cast or hammered, and the finished piece is buffed or polished. Pewterers were usually guild members, and the items they produced were stamped with their marks and frequently a mark indicating the city in which the piece was made. Domestic wares were produced of pewter, from candlesticks to drinking vessels and plates.

By the eighteenth century, special plates were used to hold the symbolic seder foods. Often, pewter plates were adapted for use during Passover by the addition of a decoration or inscription related to the festival. This plate is primarily decorated with text. The outer rim contains the order of the seder. Within are three hearts inscribed with the names of the three primary symbolic foods of the Passover seder: the matzah, the *maror* (bitter herbs), and the *Korban Pesach* (Passover offering).

Each food symbolizes a *mitzvah* (a commandment or a meritorious or benevolent act) commemorating the deliverance from slavery. When the Jews left Egypt, they did not have time to let their dough rise, hence the eating of matzah and proscription against leaven during Passover. The *maror* serves as a reminder of the bitter lives, the mental and physical anguish, of the Jews who were slaves in Egypt. The *Korban Pesach* commemorates the salvation of the Jews during the tenth plague, their exemption from the slaying of the firstborn. The Israelites were commanded (Exodus 12:21–23) to sacrifice a lamb and mark their doorposts with its blood. God would then "pass over" the door, sparing the firstborn.

Pewter, engraved.
The State Jewish Museum, Prague.

Passover Plates

Mid 19th Century
Herend, Hungary

Until the eighteenth century, the European desire for porcelain had to be satisfied with Chinese imports, which may have first reached European courts on the return of Marco Polo in the late twelfth century. True hard-paste porcelain is produced by combining clay with kaolin and firing at a temperature of approximately 1350 degrees Celsius. Although many attempts were made to duplicate Chinese hard-paste porcelain, these were unsuccessful until the early eighteenth century when experimentation resulted in the production of Meissen porcelain and the establishment of the Royal Saxon Porcelain Manufactory. Industrial piracy was not born in the twentieth century; Meissen workmen who learned the manner of production of hard-paste porcelain were in demand, highly paid to impart their knowledge to Meissen's competitors in Germany and abroad.

Moritz Fischer (1800–80) established a factory in Herend, Hungary, under the patronage of Count Charles Esterhazy and began producing hard-paste porcelain in 1839. Under Fischer, prestigious hard-paste porcelains including Sèvres, Meissen, and other popular wares were copied. Sometimes this was apparently done with intent to defraud as marks were copied as well as patterns. At other times, the patterns or color schemes might be copied, but the piece was marked to identify it as a Herend piece. Among the marks on other Herend pieces were the initials MF for Moritz Fischer and the Hungarian coat of arms.

In 1864 when the Vienna porcelain factory closed, Emperor Franz Joseph ordered that patterns for his favorite models be sent to Herend so that their production could be continued. In 1867 Fischer was given a Magyar title, Fischer of Farkashásha. On his retirement in 1873, the factory was divided among Fischer's five sons; a year later, it was bankrupt. The firm was revived in 1926.

The patron of the Sèvres porcelain factory, which dated from the mid eighteenth century, was King Louis XV (1710–74) of France. These two plates were made using popular Sèvres colors, the dark blue and gold of *bleu du Roi,* apple green, and Pompadour rose. The latter was named for Jeanne Antoinette Poisson, Marquise de Pompadour (1721–64), mistress of the king. Both plates reproduce a popular Jewish seder scene. The dark blue plate, designed in the 1840s, is dated 1854. It depicts a variant of a seder scene painted by the nineteenth-century artist Moritz Oppenheim. The pattern was revived in a limited edition produced by Herend beginning in 1980. The designer of the other plate has elaborated on a scene from the 1629 edition of the *Venice Haggadah.*

Porcelain, hand-painted.
Diameter (both): 13 in. (33 cm).
Jewish Museum, Budapest.

Majolica Seder Plate

Late 19th–Early 20th Century
Italy

Majolica describes earthenware covered with an opaque tin glaze decorated before firing. Majolica has been produced in Italy since the fifteenth century. Tin-glazed earthenware is known variously as majolica, faience, or fayence, depending upon the country of origin. Large majolica chargers, wall plaques, and figures of saints by the renowned della Robbia family are among the treasures of Italian Renaissance craftsmanship.

According to recent scholarship, this plate is one of a coherent group of twenty-eight majolica Passover plates, all of similar shape, with flanges decorated with elaborate cartouches bearing scenes, and a text (the kiddush or the order of the seder service) in the concave center. These plates are inscribed with a variety of dates and places of origin; the earliest inscribed date is 1532 and the latest 1889. Inscribed places of manufacture include Ancona, Pesaro, Padua, and Urbino.

New research has demonstrated the stylistic uniformity of this group of twenty-eight plates. The overall form and manner of depiction of various scenes is consistent which contrasts with the disparate origins and dates inscribed on the plates, indicating that these works are forgeries. The compositions of the biblical scenes found on these plates are based on the engravings of C. Kirchmayr illustrating a haggadah published in Trieste in 1864.

These majolica plates most closely resemble the ceramic wares produced in Savona and neighboring Albisola and were probably produced by the Salamone factory. A plate of this type was known to have been exhibited in London in 1887, and another example is recorded in a private collection before 1904. On the basis of this evidence, the twenty-eight plates have been dated to the period between 1864 and 1900.

The production of Judaica forgeries in the late nineteenth century indicates the growing interest in the collection of Jewish ceremonial art. The Jewish bourgeoisie in Western and Central Europe was increasingly alienated from traditional Jewish practice yet sought to preserve ties to the past. Purchasing and collecting Jewish art provided assimilated Jews with a sophisticated and distanced mode of connection with their traditional Jewish past. The growing interest in acquiring objects related to Jewish culture led to the creation of forgeries to feed an ever growing market.

Majolica.
Diameter: 16 ¾ in. (42.5 cm).
The Israel Museum, Jerusalem.
Permanent loan, Mr. and Mrs. Victor Carter,
Los Angeles, 1965.

קדוש

יום הַשִּׁשִּׁי וַיְכֻלּוּ הַשָּׁמַיִם וְהָאָרֶץ וְכָל צְבָאָם: וַיְכַל אֱלֹהִים בַּיּוֹם
הַשְּׁבִיעִי מְלַאכְתּוֹ אֲשֶׁר עָשָׂה וַיִּשְׁבֹּת בַּיּוֹם הַשְּׁבִיעִי מִכָּל מְלַאכְתּוֹ
אֲשֶׁר עָשָׂה: וַיְבָרֶךְ אֱלֹהִים אֶת יוֹם הַשְּׁבִיעִי וַיְקַדֵּשׁ אֹתוֹ כִּי בוֹ שָׁבַת מִכָּל
מְלַאכְתּוֹ אֲשֶׁר בָּרָא אֱלֹהִים לַעֲשׂוֹת: סַבְרִי מָרָנָן בָּרוּךְ אַתָּה יְיָ אֱלֹהֵינוּ
מֶלֶךְ הָעוֹלָם בּוֹרֵא פְּרִי הַגָּפֶן: בָּרוּךְ אַתָּה יְיָ אֱלֹהֵינוּ מֶלֶךְ הָעוֹלָם אֲשֶׁר
בָּחַר בָּנוּ מִכָּל עָם וְרוֹמְמָנוּ מִכָּל לָשׁוֹן וְקִדְּשָׁנוּ בְּמִצְוֹתָיו וַתִּתֶּן לָנוּ יְיָ
אֱלֹהֵינוּ בְּאַהֲבָה (שַׁבָּתוֹת לִמְנוּחָה וּ) מוֹעֲדִים לְשִׂמְחָה חַגִּים וּזְמַנִּים
לְשָׂשׂוֹן אֶת יוֹם (הַשַּׁבָּת הַזֶּה וְאֶת יוֹם) חַג הַמַּצּוֹת הַזֶּה וּזְמַן חֵרוּתֵנוּ
בְּאַהֲבָה מִקְרָא קֹדֶשׁ זֵכֶר לִיצִיאַת מִצְרָיִם כִּי בָנוּ בָחַרְתָּ וְאוֹתָנוּ קִדַּשְׁתָּ
מִכָּל הָעַמִּים (וְשַׁבָּתוֹת) וּמוֹעֲדֵי קָדְשֶׁךָ (בְּאַהֲבָה וּבְרָצוֹן) בְּשִׂמְחָה
וּבְשָׂשׂוֹן הִנְחַלְתָּנוּ בָּרוּךְ אַתָּה יְיָ מְקַדֵּשׁ (הַשַּׁבָּת וְ) יִשְׂרָאֵל וְהַזְּמַנִּים:
בָּרוּךְ אַתָּה יְיָ אֱלֹהֵינוּ מֶלֶךְ הָעוֹלָם בּוֹרֵא מְאוֹרֵי הָאֵשׁ: בָּרוּךְ אַתָּה
יְיָ אֱלֹהֵינוּ מֶלֶךְ הָעוֹלָם שֶׁהֶחֱיָנוּ וְקִיְּמָנוּ וְהִגִּיעָנוּ לַזְּמַן הַזֶּה:

קַדֵּשׁ . וּרְחַץ . כַּרְפַּס . יַחַץ . מַגִּיד .
רָחְצָה . מוֹצִיא מַצָּה . מָרוֹר .
כּוֹרֵךְ . שֻׁלְחָן עוֹרֵךְ . צָפוּן .
בָּרֵךְ . הַלֵּל . נִרְצָה .

Brass Seder Plate

Late 19th Century

Jerusalem

One of the most popular songs of the Passover seder rite is *Had Gadya*. The song, written in Aramaic and sung at the conclusion of the seder, is composed of ten stanzas. Each stanza recapitulates in reverse order the text of the previous stanzas. The final stanza reads "Then came the Holy One, praised be He, and slew the Angel of Death who slew the slaughterer who slaughtered the ox that drank the water that quenched the fire that burned the stick that hit the dog that bit the cat that ate the kid that father bought for two zuzim." The ten stanzas of the song are a prominent feature in the decoration of this copper seder plate. Around the inside of the plate is a series of ten heptagonal cartouches containing scenes from the ten stanzas of *Had Gadya*. The cartouche to the left of the uppermost interior cartouche portrays the first stanza, a man leading a kid. The song then continues counterclockwise, concluding with the uppermost cartouche.

A series of oval cartouches around the outer portion of the plate, beginning with the uppermost cartouche and continuing counterclockwise, contains pictures of the portions of the seder up to the meal itself. Inside the circle formed by these cartouches is a circular inscription of the text of Exodus 12:42: "That was for the Lord a night of vigil to bring them out of the land of Egypt; that same night is the Lord's, one of vigil for all the children of Israel throughout the ages." The center of the plate shows two pillars and a candelabrum. Arching above the pillars and below the floral design is the Hebrew inscription *siman l'seder shel Pesah,* "sign (mnemonic device) for the Passover seder." Between the pillars is the inscription "A story is told about Rabbi Eliezer and Rabbi Joshua and Rabbi Elazar ben Azariah and Rabbi . . . who were reclining in B'nai B'rak and telling the going forth from Egypt." Seated between the pillars are three of the rabbis named in this portion of the seder story. Inscribed into the base of the pillars is the passage "The more one tells of the going forth from [Egypt] the more praiseworthy he is."

Inlaid or engraved copper and brass wares were very popular in the Middle East due to the influence of Ottoman metalwork traditions. The spectacular metalwork crafted during the Mamluk period (1250–1517) was emulatd during the stylistic period known as the Mamluk revival (1878-1914). In Islamic countries Jews frequently worked as metalsmiths because the *Koran* condemns the hoarding of precious metals, and pious Muslims frequently avoided this profession. Jewish ceremonial objects were crafted in Jerusalem not only for use by the local community but also as souvenirs for travelers and as presentation pieces for patrons of Jerusalem-based institutions.

Brass, engraved.
Michael Kaniel Judaica Collection, Jerusalem.

Tiered Seder Set

18th–19th Century
Poland

This is a unique example of an exuberant, folk-inspired three-tiered seder set. Many examples of nineteenth-century seder sets featuring three tiers of plates to hold the matzahs and containers for ceremonial foods are known. Most other seder sets were crafted of silver in Germany or Austria or were made of pewter or other base metals. The combination of brass and wood in this example from Poland is unusual.

The set features many elements typical of the energetic nature of Polish Jewish folk art. The frequent use of animal motifs (birds, stags, or most often lions, the symbol of the tribe of Judah) is a characteristic trait of Polish Jewish folk art. Although the combination of brass and wood is unusual, both materials are typical of folk Judaica from this region.

Polish Jewish woodcarvers were famed for their elaborate and often eccentric creations. Torah arks featured complex carvings of twisted columns and floral or animal motifs and were often crowned by a decalogue with flanking lions. The arrangement of the lions flanking cartouches in this seder set, with mouths agape, arched backs, and sinuously curved tails, is reminiscent of these carved Torah arks. Smaller ceremonial objects, usually Torah pointers, were also carved from wood. In Poland woodcarvers also created wooden grave markers featuring elaborate interlace and animal motifs. Exuberant brass Hanukkah lamps were frequently used in Poland and typically featured animal motifs and grillwork, elements also found here. The notched motif seen in the apertures of the grillwork in this set is echoed in the detailed paws of the lions.

This seder set formerly belonged to the Jewish Community of Danzig (now Gdansk, Poland). In 1939 leaders of the Jewish community of Danzig, recognizing the increased threat posed by the Nazis, shipped this and more than 250 other ceremonial objects to New York. The Danzig community specified that if after fifteen years there were no Jews remaining in Danzig, the collection would remain in America to educate and inspire the rest of the world. The shipment from Danzig's Jewish community arrived in New York on July 26, 1939; on August 31st, 1939, the German army marched into Danzig.

Brass, cast, cut out, engraved; wood, painted and stained; ink on paper; silk, embroidered; linen; cotton.
13 ¾ × 14 in. (35 × 35.5 cm).
The Jewish Museum, New York.
Gift of the Danzig Jewish Community.

Silver Tiered Seder Plate

1815

Vienna, Austria

This three-tiered silver seder plate is an example of an elaborate type which graced the seder tables of affluent nineteenth-century Viennese Jewish families. The three tiers are designed to hold the three ceremonial matzahs. Small rings on the outer rail surrounding the upper surface held a curtain around the plate to cover the matzahs. The plate is supported by eagle-shaped feet. The containers for the ceremonial food are crafted as complete figures bearing vessels. Moses, the largest figure, stands prominently in the center of the plate, balancing a holder for the Cup of Elijah on his head.

The market for silver pieces expanded during the nineteenth century, partly in response to the mechanized production of the Industrial Revolution which made available a greater number of less expensive pieces. Decorative elements on silver drew from the decorative vocabulary of sculpture and wall and vase paintings from ancient Greece and Rome. These motifs had been popular since the time of the French Revolution and continued in vogue through the early nineteenth century. While nineteenth-century pieces borrow general details of costume and ornament from Greco-Roman works, they would rarely be mistaken for originals.

The use of complete three-dimensional human figures in Jewish ceremonial art is unusual, as representations of this type were frequently seen to violate the commandment against graven images. A contemporary discussion of Jewish legal attitudes towards the use of human figures in ceremonial art is that of Rabbi Moses Sofer of Pressburg (1762–1839). He states that figures on a Torah shield could not be considered potential objects of worship because the identities of the figures (Moses and Aaron) were clearly established by their manner of dress. It is important to note that the figures on Torah shields were not complete sculpture in the round, as is the case in the seder plates of this type. Earlier Jewish ritual objects incorporating figural decoration survive, including German eighteenth-century spice containers, *havdalah* candleholders, and hanging lamps. The many Viennese seder plates with figures bearing ceremonial foods indicate the popular acceptance of the use of human figures in ritual art.

It is likely that rabbis, patrons, and artists were more comfortable with the use of figures in objects crafted for home ritual, such as the seder, and more frequently avoided such representations in objects for the synagogue, where the suggestion of idolatrous worship was more likely.

Silver, cast, engraved.
Hebrew Union College Skirball Museum, Los Angeles.

Repoussé Tiered Seder Plate

c. 1872
Vienna, Austria

Begining in the late eighteenth-century and especially in the first decades of the nineteenth century, Vienna became a center of the *Haskalah* (Enlightenment) movement which encouraged increased emancipation, secular learning, and religious reform among Jews. The importance and influence of Vienna's Jewish community greatly increased following Austria's annexation of Galicia in 1772.

During the second half of the nineteenth century and the first decades of the twentieth century, Vienna's Jewish population grew due to the immigration of Jews from other regions of the Austrian empire, particularly in Galicia, Hungary, and Bukovina. Before the Holocaust there were fifty-nine places of worship in Vienna representing various branches of Judaism. A strong educational network existed. A "Pedagogium" provided training for Hebrew teachers. The rabbinical seminary founded in 1893 was a center for research in Jewish history and literature. The city was the home to many Jewish charitable and relief organizations, including the Rothschild Hospital and three orphanages. Despite strong opposition by segments of the community, Vienna was also a major center of Zionist activity. Theodor Herzl published *Die Welt,* the official organ of the Zionist movement in Vienna.

The ornate silver seder plate shown here was made in Vienna around 1870. It stands on four conch feet, and two eagles serve as handles on the sides. A green glass gem adorns the ornamental handle on top of the piece. The three gilt shelves to hold the ceremonial matzahs are accessible through two hinged doors that open the width of one side of the plate. On each door, a pair of lions supports the tablets of the Ten Commandments beneath a crown, a common motif in Jewish ceremonial art. Flowering branches also decorate the doors. The top of the plate is bordered by a railing of leaves and fleurs-de-lys.

Five containers in the shape of wheelbarrows, a bucket, and other vessels serve to hold the symbolic foods. Ceremonial vessels often heighten the symbolism of the foods eaten at the seder. *Haroset* recalls the mortar used by the slaves in Egypt and is presented on this seder plate in a container shaped like a wheelbarrow. The incongruity of implements of servitude, such as buckets and wheelbarrows, being crafted of precious metal parallels the juxtaposition of slavery and freedom, a recurring theme of the seder service.

The use of eagles as decorative motifs, as found on this seder plate, was widespread. The eagle was the symbol of imperial Rome and was also used as an imperial symbol by Napoleon and the Habsburgs. The eagle symbol in the context of the seder service is particularly appropriate, recalling the biblical verse describing the exodus from Egypt: "You have seen what I did to the Egyptians, how I bore you on eagles' wings and brought you to Me" (Exodus 19.4).

Makers: L. & L. Mandl, Vormals Pills & Co.
Silver, cast, repoussé, engraved, gilt, glass.
10 ½ × 18 ¼ in. (27 × 46.4 cm).
The Israel Museum, Jerusalem. Feuchtwanger Collection, purchased and donated by Baruch and Ruth Rappaport, Geneva, 1969.

Tiered Seder Plate and Elijah Cup

20th Century

Friedrich Adler

Objects produced for Jewish festivals are eclectic, drawing on contemporary forms prevalent in the area in which they are produced, as well as traditional motifs.

Before the twentieth century it was unusual to find cups made especially to function as the cup placed on the seder table for Elijah; a family would use its largest or most precious cup. During the twentieth century a number of artists have designed special cups for this purpose.

Friedrich Adler (1870–1942) trained at the Academy of Arts and Crafts in Munich. For a time, he was associated with the Lehr- und Versuch-Ateliers für Angewandte und Freie Kunst (known as the Debschitz School), a group working in the *Jugendstil* idiom (the German variant of Art Nouveau). His metalwork received prizes at exhibitions in Turin (1902), St. Louis (1904), and Brussels (1910). Perhaps under the dual influence of his arts and crafts background and contemporary currents, he altered his style slightly, bringing it closer to Wiener Werkstatte production, distinguished by grid-like designs, and sharp geometric motifs.

Adler exhibited in 1914 at the Deutsche Werkbund Exhibition in Cologne with Walter Gropius (1883-1969) and other modernists later connected with the Bauhaus. The aim of the Bauhaus school, founded in 1919 by Gropius, was to produce well-designed objects with simple forms, capable of being mass-produced yet reflecting individual fine craftsmanship. All elements of the environment, from the architectural style of the building to the furniture, textiles, and domestic objects were to harmonize.

Bauhaus promoted an esthetic based on functionalism and simple geometric form. Decorative elements are kept to a minimum. Lettering, like that decorating the tray and wine cups, is clean, clear, and simple.

Friedrich Adler taught at the Academy in Hamburg until the National Socialists came to power in 1933. At that time, he was forced to leave the Academy because he was a Jew. Deported to Auschwitz in 1942, Adler was never heard from again.

The square form of this three-tiered container for matzah attests to the effects of industrialization on traditional form. By the end of the nineteenth century, matzah was mass-produced and cut into squares. While earlier pieces combining a tray for the ceremonial food with separate tiers for each of the three matzahs were round, such as the example from Danzig, the lower section of Adler's piece is square to accommodate the shape of contemporary matzah.

Seder plate: silver, embossed and cut-out, glass insert.
Height: 4 in. (10.2 cm); diameter: 17 5/16 in. (44 cm).

Cup of Elijah: silver-plated, repoussé and cut-out, moonstones.
Height: 9 11/16 in. (25 cm); diameter (rim): 6 1/16 in. (15.4 cm).

Both: The Spertus Museum of Judaica, Chicago, Illinois.

Seder Plate

1934
Alois Wörle

On November 9, 1918, a new government was proclaimed in Germany, and two days later the Germans signed an armistice, ending World War I. In 1919 the German National Assembly met in Weimar, a city in central Germany, to establish the Weimar Republic. The choice of Weimar was a deliberate break with the past and was intended to offer hope for a brighter future, a hope that was destined to fail. The harsh terms of the Treaty of Versailles, imposed on Germany by the victorious Allies, left a bitterness in Germany that would bring the world once again to war.

Art, as well as politics, saw changes in 1919. During the same year, in Weimar, the architect Walter Gropius founded the Bauhaus school of design, an idea he conceived during active service at the front.

The central idea of the Bauhaus was to synthesize craftsmanship, design, and technology to give architects, painters, and sculptors a practical place in society. The techniques of industrial production were studied, and many student projects were actually prototypes for mass production.

The influence of the Bauhaus spread throughout the world but not without opposition. At the beginning of 1933, Adolph Hitler became Chancellor of Germany, ended the Weimar Republic, and closed the Bauhaus. Although the Bauhaus was closed because of Hitler's hatred for modern art and architecture, its influence remained.

Once in power, Hitler began to put into effect laws that gradually took away the rights of the Jews. The city of Munich, the birthplace of the Nazi party and known as the "capital of the movement," had a Jewish population of about 9,000 in 1933. By 1938, records show that 3,574 Jews had left the city; of these, 3,130 went abroad. During the same period there were 803 deaths and only 118 births. The death of the Weimar Republic and of the Bauhaus was now being paralleled by the death of the Jewish community.

As if in protest, Alois Wörle, active as a silversmith in Munich during the twenties and thirties, produced this impressive copper and brass seder plate in 1934. The influence of the Bauhaus school is manifest in the visible structural elements and clean, simple lines of the plate. The plate rests on feet that are plain disks. Structural elements such as the brass rivets that hold the top and bottom to the central copper container are visible, rather than being hidden as they are in many of the older tiered seder plates, and become integral parts of the design.

Copper was less expensive than silver and a popular material with craftsmen at this time. It gives a warm appearance and is extremely malleable. In this piece, the copper itself becomes a decorative element.

Several aspects of this seder plate are traditional. Three shelves inside hold the ceremonial matzahs; access is gained by doors that slide open along an interior track. The octagonal top holds containers with glass inserts for the symbolic foods. The inscription around the plate is from the haggadah; "This is the bread of affliction our ancestors ate in the Land of Egypt."

Copper, brass, and glass.
Height: 7 in. (18 cm); diameter: 13 ¾ in. (35 cm).
Gift of Harry Weinberg in memory of Fanny Weinberg and her son Nathan. The Israel Museum, Jerusalem.

Terezín Seder Plate

1944
Terezín (Theresienstadt)

In 1938, under the Munich Agreement, Czechoslovakia was forced to cede the Sudetenland area of the province of Bohemia to Germany. At this time, the Jewish population in Czech lands numbered 122,000. On March 14, 1939, Slovakia, under the direction of Andrej Hlinka's People's Party, declared its independence from Prague, the Czech capital, and signed a Treaty of Protection with Nazi Germany. On March 15, 1939, German troops occupied the country and transformed the area into a German protectorate. From the occupation in March 1939 until the establishment of the concentration camp ghetto in Terezín in October 1941, approximately 26,000 Jews emigrated to Palestine, the United States, South America, and Western Europe. Of the remaining 92,000 Jews, approximately 74,000 were forced to occupy the camp at Terezín. Over 80 percent of the Terezín deportees were eventually deported to extermination camps, such as Auschwitz, Maidanek, Treblinka, and Sobibor. Researchers in postwar Czechoslovakia, working from actual transport records, have calculated that 77,297 Czechoslovakian Jews were killed by the Nazis.

Terezín (Theresienstadt), a medieval fortress town in Bohemia, was designated by the Nazis to be a settlement for the concentration of most of the Jewish population of Bohemia and Moravia, together with privileged, famous, or elderly Jews from Germany and elsewhere in Western Europe. According to Nazi plan, the Terezín ghetto was to be a transfer point—the inhabitants to be gradually sent to extermination camps. The Nazis hoped to conceal the systematic extermination of European Jewry and to use Terezín as a model settlement. An International Red Cross investigation team toured an artifically sanitized and beautified Terezín in July of 1944. Additional deportations to Auschwitz reduced the overcrowded conditions before the Red Cross visit. A bank, café, shop, and schools were set up, and flower gardens were planted in the ghetto to impress the Red Cross inspectors.

Jewish leaders responsible for much of the organization and administration of the ghetto were greatly concerned with the education of young people. In children's homes, where most school-age children lived, instructors managed to maintain a normal curriculum. Many artists, writers, and scholars had been deported to Terezín and organized an extensive program of performances, lectures, and study in the ghetto. The cultural and educational achievements in the Terezín ghetto are outstanding manifestations of spiritual resistance under Nazi rule.

This three-tiered seder plate is inscribed in German: "The Jewish Youth Movement to the Jewish Council of Elders, Theresienstadt, April 3, 1944." The freedom from enslavement celebrated at Passover must have been a powerful symbol of hope for the ill-fated Jewish community of the Terezín ghetto in the spring of 1944.

Wood inscribed with ink and stained; cotton reinforced with copper wire.
Diameter: 6 ½ × 12 ½ in. (16.5 × 32 cm).
The State Jewish Museum, Prague.

Tiered Seder Plate: From Slavery to Freedom

1990

Lorelei and Alex Gruss

Lorelei and Alex Gruss are a husband and wife artistic team collaborating on the production of inlaid ceremonial art. Lorelei was born in New York, and at the age of 15 began to apprentice in Jerusalem for various craftsmen, developing skills in woodworking and silversmithing. Alex was born in Buenos Aires, Argentina, and emigrated to Israel as a teenager. He worked in Israeli television as a graphic and stage designer and as a cartoonist and illustrator for many publications in Israel and the United States. In 1984 Lorelei and Alex were married in Jerusalem and since 1988 have been working as a team to create inlaid ceremonial objects.

Artists have created outstanding examples of carved and inlaid wooden Judaica for centuries. Eastern European wood-carvers created elaborate synagogue arks, frequently massive constructions with twisted columns and rampant animal figures. Smaller objects such as Torah pointers, and even tombstones, were also frequently crafted of wood. Wood inlay often decorated the staves of the Torah scroll. In Sefardic communities, a rigid wood case for the Torah scroll, a *tik,* was often decorated with inlay of mother-of-pearl or ivory. These Torah cases were frequently twelve-sided, as is this seder tray, and symbolically alluded to the twelve tribes of Israel.

Lorelei and Alex Gruss have used the characteristics of the various inlay materials to heighten the impact of their compositions. As the Israelites proceed from slavery to freedom, they also proceed from darkness to light. In the first panel the hues are subtle, and in the last panel the radiance of the Holy Land is expressed with a sun of 14-karat gold. The waves and eddies of the Red Sea are conveyed with the concentric, spiral patterns of abalone. Sections of wood inlay were carefully selected and positioned so that linear wood grain patterns complement the composition of the scene.

The inscription from the haggadah on the twelve panels of this seder tray, "in every generation, each man must regard himself as though he, himself, had come out from Egypt," serves as a thematic leitmotif for this finely crafted ceremonial object. One word of this twelve-word Hebrew phrase is inscribed on each panel of this three-tiered seder tray. The artists have conveyed the exodus from Egypt as interconnected to the millenia of Jewish history. Throughout, the scenes depicted on the seder tray seem to be historically inaccurate juxtapositions. The depiction of the Jews leaving Egypt includes a Russian Jew, with valise in hand, who is shown among the freed slaves and ancient pyramids. A Polish Hasid is a spectator at the drowning of the Egyptian army in the Red Sea. The never-ending process of redemption is expressed through these anachronistic elements. Among the Israelites entering the land of Israel is a lone Jew wearing a striped concentration camp uniform emblazoned with a yellow star, a reference to the slavery of the Holocaust preceding the establishment of the State of Israel. The final scene depicts Jerusalem, and thus corresponds to the final statement of the seder night—"Next year in Jerusalem." The first and last panel of the seder tray are joined to indicate the continuous cycle of Jewish history and experience.

Ebony, purpleheart, silver. Inlay: padauk, cocobolo, maple, imboya, osage Orange; pink ivory; mahogany; vera wood; mother-of-pearl; abalone; shells; silver; brass; copper; antique ivory; gemstones; gold.
18 × 10 in. (45.7 × 25.4 cm).
One of an edition of 10.
Private Collection.

Beaker

End, 19th Century
Germany

The section of the haggadah that speaks of the Four Sons is frequently decorated with figures representing the sons. They symbolize children of various attitudes and abilities. Although the text of the haggadah says that the Torah speaks of four sons, they are only described indirectly. It is through the interpretive process known as *midrash* that the text reveals the four sons.

The story of the four sons arises out of the differences in language in four places in the Torah. The wise son is hinted at in Deuteronomy 6:20: "When, in time to come, your children ask you, 'What mean the decrees, laws, and rules that the Lord our God has commanded you?'" This son is considered wise because he uses three Hebrew terms regarding the observance of the holiday—he is obviously concerned with all the details.

The wicked son is hinted at in Exodus 12:26: "And when your children ask you, 'What do you mean by this rite?'" This son has not asked about details as has the wise son; he has only used language of exclusion—what does it mean to *you*? While it is true that the wise son said "commanded you," seeming to use the language of exclusion used by the wicked son, he also used language of inclusion—"The Lord *our* God"—as well as concerning himself with the details.

The simple son is alluded to in Exodus 13:14: "And when, in time to come, your son asks you, saying, 'What does this mean?'" The question asked here is very simple. It does not ask for details and it does not ask for meaning. It asks a very basic question—obviously prompted by the son noticing that something is different.

The son who does not know how to ask is implied in Exodus 13:8: "And you shall explain to your son on that day." No question has been asked here, and this differentiates this son from the other three. In the other three instances, a question is asked and an answer is given.

The cup shown here depicts one of the four sons on each of its main faces. The figures are based on those drawn by Avram bar Ya'akov for the first *Amsterdam Haggadah* which in turn were borrowed from *Icones Biblicae* by Matthew Merian. In the Merian image, the figure chosen to depict the wise son was part of a scene depicting Hannibal offering a sacrifice. The wise son, visible in this view and identified below the image, is bearded and wears a turban and long cloak.

The shape of this piece, one without stem or handle, is known as a beaker derived from the shape of animal horns used as early drinking vessels. The shape and name both originated in Scandinavia and spread to coastal towns of England and Europe and from there to all countries in the West. Beakers were often fluted, as seen here. Arabesques and scrolled foliage were common ornamental motifs.

Silver, repoussé, partial gilding.
6 ½ x 3 ¾ in. (16.5 x 9.5 cm).
The Israel Museum, Jerusalem.
Lent by Mr. and Mrs. Victor Carter, California, 1965.

Silver Gilt Goblet

18th Century

Warsaw

This lavish silver gilt goblet features an engraved Hebrew inscription, a quote from the haggadah: "These are the ten plagues with which the Holy One, blessed be He, punished the Egyptians." The large size of this goblet and its elaborate decoration suggest that it may have been used as an Elijah cup.

The upper section of the goblet is decorated with ten interlocking raised teardrops, each portraying one of the ten plagues in high relief repoussé.

Depictions of the ten plagues were common in illustrated haggadahs. Miniatures illustrating individual plagues can be found in many medieval illuminated manuscripts. The first composite arrangement of scenes depicting all ten plagues appeared in the famed *Venice Haggadah* of 1609 whose innovative illustrations were used as models for many later printed and manuscript haggadahs. The depictions of all ten plagues on this goblet are probably based on similar scenes in a printed haggadah and can be linked to the tradition established by the *Venice Haggadah*.

The first explicit evidence of Jewish settlement in Warsaw dates from 1414. Jews were expelled from Warsaw in 1483, and the Jewish population remained small for centuries. In 1796 Warsaw came under Prussian control, and Jewish immigrants from Prussia, Silesia, and elsewhere flocked to the city. Throughout the early nineteenth century, Warsaw's Jewish population grew at such a rapid pace that it became Europe's largest Jewish community and a center for a variety of religious, cultural, and intellectual activities.

When Nazi forces entered Warsaw on September 29, 1939, there were 393,950 Jews. On January 17, 1945, the city was liberated. On that day only 200 Jewish survivors were found in underground hiding places in the ruins of the city.

Silver, gilt, embossed, engraved.
7 ⅞ × 4 ⅛ in. (20 × 10.5 cm).
Jewish Museum, Budapest.
Hallmark: Warsaw (Rosenberg IV, no. 8119).

Ivory Beaker

18th Century

Germany

Throughout the ages ivory has been a favorite medium for carvers. Extremely durable, it is receptive to many techniques of carving. Able to be carved into delicate shapes, it easily shows very fine lines and can be used to produce miniatures as well as larger items. The final product is limited only by the size of the piece of ivory available to the carver, his artistic skill, and the quality of the source.

The beauty of ivory was celebrated in the "Song of Songs": "His belly is a tablet of ivory, adorned with sapphires" (5:14) and "Your neck is like a tower of ivory" (7:5). Ivory was rare and expensive, a sign of opulence. King Solomon had "a great throne of ivory, and overlaid it with the finest gold" (I Kings 10:18). King Ahab had an "ivory palace" (I Kings 22:39). The prophet Amos railed against those who ". . . lie on ivory beds" (6:4).

The beauty and luxurious nature of ivory have been popular in many cultures and ages. It was usually painted with many hues including gold and prized by kings and nobles as a symbol of wealth and status.

The Hebrew inscription states that the cup was carved by Yosef ben Yitzhak. The carving portrays Moses and Aaron beseeching the pharaoh to allow the Israelite slaves to go free. The text carved around the top of the cup says *Shelah et ami*, "Let my people go (Exodus 5:1)." Also carved on the cup are scenes from the life of Joseph including Joseph as viceroy to the pharaoh and Joseph with Potiphar's wife.

The story of Joseph's deliverance has been used on many occasions throughout history to prefigure redemption. Events from his life decorate items as diverse as catacomb paintings, ivory carvings used as chairs and book bindings, and mosaics. Extended narrative cycles depicting the story of Joseph can be found in many diverse places, among them the earliest extant illuminated manuscripts, including the *Vienna Genesis* attributed to sixth-century Syria; Coptic textiles dated to the eighth century; cylindrical ivory containers, a shape known as a pyxis; catacomb paintings in the Via Latina, Rome, attributed to the fourth century C.E.; and thirteenth-century mosaics in the cupola of Saint Mark's, Venice.

Certain events are depicted in these examples which have only been traced to Jewish literature, and some of these early cycles of depictions are extensive. This has lead some art historians to postulate the existence of an early illustrated Jewish version of the Bible or of collections of legends that were copied for these non-Jewish versions.

Carved ivory.
Height: 3 $^{11}/_{16}$ in. (9.5 cm); diameter: 2 $^{5}/_{16}$ in. (6 cm).
Sir Isaac and Lady Edith Wolfson Museum,
Hechal Shlomo, Jerusalem.

glass manufacture were found in Israel in the Jewish Quarter of the Old City of Jerusalem and in Ein Gedi and date to the first century B.C.E. Glass has been used for drinking vessels since the Roman period.

The Industrial Revolution of the nineteenth century made a great amount of glassware accessible to the general population. Inexpensive glassware became more readily available, and glass manufacturing processes allowed for large-scale production of delicate items that had previously required highly skilled craftsmen. A vast variety of decorated glass was produced, including both functional and decorative glassware. Much of the glass produced during the nineteenth century was made in Germany and Bohemia. The engraved decoration of glassware during this period included such diverse subjects as city scenes, landscapes, hunting scenes, and portraits. Engravers also produced specially commissioned items.

By the nineteenth century, glassmakers could emulate elaborate engraving with acid-etching which gave the surface a matte finish. The surface was flux-coated with wax or another acid-resistant substance, and a stylus was used to draw the desired pattern in the wax. Then, acid was applied to the glass, etching

been used for luxurious drinking vessels since the sixteenth century. The scene depicted on the clear glass goblet from the Max Berger collection appears to be based on a painted or engraved version of a well-known nineteenth-century painting of a seder scene by Moritz Oppenheim.

The goblet from the Spertus collection also depicts a Passover seder scene. Its purpose is specifically stated in its decoration, as it is inscribed "Cup of Elijah." It is believed that Elijah the Prophet visits Jewish homes during the seder and will some day usher in the Messiah.

Left: Cup of Elijah.
Glass, blown and cut.
Height: 7 ¼ in. (18.4 cm.); diameter (rim): 3 ⅛ in. (7.9 cm).
The Spertus Museum of Judaica, Chicago, Illinois.
Gift of Mr. and Mrs. Philip Pinsof.

Right: Goblet.
Glass, blown and cut.
Collection of Max Berger.

Cup of Elijah

1989

Michel Schwartz

This magnificent Cup of Elijah was made by Michel Schwartz (1926–) of Brooklyn, New York, an artist well known for the elegant Hebrew lettering in his works.

The beaker is constructed in several sections: the inscribed outer sheath, a removable inner beaker, and the pedestal. The inscription contains more than 700 letters meticulously cut by hand using jewelers' saws. The Hebrew inscription is a *zemer,* an ancient song of praise dedicated to the prophet Elijah read at the end of Sabbath after sunset, *Eliyahu Ha-Navi* ("Elijah, the Prophet"). The song is composed of eleven stanzas and a refrain. The first letter of the second word in the first twenty-two sentences of the song form an acrostic using the twenty-two letters of the Hebrew alphabet.

The text of the song refers to Elijah's zeal in the defense of God's name and his expected role as the one who will bring the good tidings of the coming of the Messiah. And it recalls that Elijah is expected to bring about peace between parents and children and will settle all outstanding scholarly disputes about issues of Jewish law.

The base is inscribed "When it was time to present the meal offering, the prophet Elijah came forward and said, 'O Lord, God of Abraham, Isaac, and Israel, let it be known today that You are God in Israel and that I am Your servant, and that I have done all these things at Your bidding.'" "The hand of the Lord had come upon Elijah. He girded his loins and ran in front of Ahab all the way to Jezreel." (I Kings 18:36, 46). The letters of the inscription were cut by hand and then surface-polished to give the saucer a two-tone gold-silver finish.

In 1990 Michel and Josepha Schwartz and Jack and Belle Rosenbaum presented the cup to Rabbi Menachem M. Schneerson, the Lubavitcher Rebbe, in honor of his eighty-eighth birthday. The artist proudly states that, "From the day the Rebbe received this cup to this very day, it has never left his presence for a moment, day or night."

Cup: 9 ½ × 3 ¾ in. (24.1 × 9.5 cm).
Saucer: 1 × 6 ½ in. (2.5 × 16.5 cm).
Silver and 24K gold.
Private collection.

Ewer and Basin

1849–50

Istanbul

Hands are washed ritually twice during the seder service—without a blessing before eating *karpas,* the green vegetable, and with a blessing before eating matzah. This elegant ewer and basin were used for ritual handwashing during the seder service by the Benguiat family of Izmir (Smyrna). Hadji Ephraim Benguiat was an antiquities dealer and collector. His Judaica was exhibited at the World Columbia Exhibition in Chicago in 1892–93 and later deposited at the Smithsonian Institution. In 1925 the collection was acquired by the Jewish Theological Seminary and comprised the nucleus of the Judaica collection of the Jewish Museum of New York. The name of the original owner, Ahmad Pasha Karim ibn Sharif, is engraved in Ottoman characters on the ewer handle and on the upper surface of the basin. The inscription also includes the Muslim year 1266, the equivalent of 1849–50. Sometime after this date, the set was acquired by the Benguiat family.

This ewer and basin are crafted of tombac, a zinc or copper alloy (copper in this case), gilt to a high luster. Highly prized by the sultan's court in the sixteenth century, tombac remained popular through the nineteenth century. The ewer and basin are both covered with an undulating repeat pattern of sinuous trees on a hill. The serpentine forms of the repoussé decoration echo the elegant curves of the ewer's body, handle, spout, and the gentle flare of the basin's broad rim. Elegant, stylized floral motifs were a speciality of Ottoman craftsmen, inspired both by the Muslim prohibition against figural representation and by the sultan's beautiful gardens.

The elegant shape of this ewer and basin and the rhythmic interplay of light and shadow are testimony to the artistry of Ottoman metalsmiths. The polished tree and hill motifs are set against a matte punched ground, heightening the rich luster of the gilt surface. Ewers and basins were used in the Ottoman Empire for both ritual and domestic purposes and were crafted in both base and precious metals.

Ottoman Jewry flourished following the expulsion of the Jews from Spain in 1492. Sultan Bayazid II (c. 1447–1512) actively encouraged the immigration of Sefardic refugees. The Ottoman Empire grew dramatically in the next generations encouraged by the impetus of new technology, such as printing and armaments brought from Spain, and by the financial expertise of Sefardic bankers such as the Nasi family.

In the period when this ewer and basin were crafted, Jewish life flourished in Izmir. Sultan Mahmoud II (1808–38) appointed the first *haham bashi* (chief rabbi) of Izmir in 1836, confirming official recognition of the Jewish community and granting it equal status with the Armenian and Greek Orthodox communities of the Ottoman Empire.

This ewer and basin are emblematic of the frequent practice in Jewish families of adopting decorative objects created for the surrounding culture and using them to beautify Jewish ritual. Objects created within an Islamic culture, generally devoid of figural forms, were particularly well-suited for use in a Jewish ceremonial context.

Copper, (tombac), gilt, repoussé, punched and engraved.
Ewer: 12 ¾ × 8 ½ in. (32.4 × 21.6 cm).
Basin: 4 ⅞ × 14 ½ in. (12.3 × 36.8 cm) diameter.
The Jewish Museum, New York.
The H. Ephraim and Mordecai Benguiat Family Collection.

Search for Leaven/L'Examen du Levain

1733

Bernard Picart

Bernard Picart (1673–1733) was a French Protestant who moved to Amsterdam in 1710 to find the freedom he lacked in Catholic France during the reign of Louis XIV (1638–1715). His sketches of Jewish life in Amsterdam include life-cycle events from circumcision to death and various holidays celebrated both in the synagogue and at home. Picart produced 600 illustrations for the Amsterdam publisher J.F. Bernard's *Cérémonies et coutumes religieuses de tous les peuples du monde.*

Here we see the ritual of *bedikat hametz* carried out in accordance with the proscription against having any leaven in a Jewish home during Passover (Exodus 12:15). The caption under the print, in both English and French, describes the ritual. After the home has been completely cleaned of leaven (*hametz*), several symbolic crumbs of bread are placed throughout the house on the night before Passover. The house must then be searched for the leaven which is gathered to demonstrate that the dwelling is now indeed clean of *hametz*. The *hametz* will be burned the following day.

This scene is set in the kitchen of a fashionable Jewish home in eighteenth-century Amsterdam. The contents of a cabinet have been removed so that the father can sweep the shelf for crumbs while his son holds a candle. Members of the family are stylishly dressed. The father wears a banyan, an informal caftan-like garment, and a turban. One of the children holds a hobbyhorse. Their home and garments demonstrate the importance of general social and economic factors, rather than religious ones, as determinants of fashion in dress, domestic interiors, and even toys in the global culture of the capitals of Europe during the eighteenth century.

There was a strong tradition of genre painting in Holland, depicting scenes apparently taken from daily life but chosen to illustrate a particular moral, frequently that of the vanity of earthly pleasures. During the late 1600s, genre scenes became popular for their own sake. At this time, a number of illustrated works on ethnography were produced, including anthologies of Jewish customs. The earliest of these was *Philologus Hebraeo Mixtus* in 1663 by the Calvinist theologian Johann Leusden (1624–99), who taught Hebrew at the University of Utrecht.

There also existed a Jewish tradition of books illustrating Jewish customs and ceremonies (*minhagim*); non-Jewish sources also describe and illustrate such practices. The earliest known examples dating from the sixteenth century. Picart was probably familiar with these works, but his renditions of the scenes are fresh visions, possibly taken from scenes he had viewed rather than copies of earlier examples. Picart's original drawings are in the Fodor Museum in Amsterdam.

Many Jews who fled the Inquisition in Spain and Portugal in the fifteenth and sixteenth centuries went to the Netherlands where they were permitted to worship in peace, to own land, and enjoy other rights and privileges denied them elsewhere. Here they had no fear of expulsion or exploitation by extra taxation, were not required to wear garments identifying them as Jews or restricted to specific professions. The Jewish community of the Netherlands prospered in this climate of religious and economic freedom.

Engraver: Claude du Bosc. From *The Ceremonies and Religious Customs of the Various Nations of the Known World,* Vol. I. Colored etching.
5 ¾ × 7 ¾ in. (14.6 × 18.6 cm).
Private collection.

THE SEARCH for the LEAVEN &c.

A The Mistress of the family puts Leavened Bread in various
places, to the end that her Husband in his search may find it.

L'EXAMEN du LEVAIN &c.

A La Maitresse de la maison, qui met du PAIN LEVÉ en divers
endroits, afin que son Mari qui en fait la recherche en trouve.

The Fire Came and Burnt the Stick

1919

El Lissitzky

El Lissitzky (1890–1941) was born Lazar Markowich in Smolensk, Russia. He trained as an architect in Darmstadt from 1909 to 1914, after being refused admission to the art academy in St. Petersburg because he was Jewish. He later worked as an architect in Moscow. In 1916, The Jewish Ethnographic Society financed expeditions by Lissitzky and the artist Issachar Ryback to explore the art and architecture of the wooden synagogues along the Dnieper River. Lissitzky's reminiscences reveal that he was overwhelmed by this experience.

Lissitzky, like many artists of his circle such as Nathan Altman and Marc Chagall, sought to create a modern Jewish art style. These artists combined elements derived from Jewish folk art sources with a modern art vocabulary. Lissitzky's art simultaneously served Jewish nationalism and the Russian Revolution. In his illustrations and book designs for Yiddish children's books he experimented with new artistic forms of the Hebrew alphabet and with cubo-futurist compositions. Lissitzky designed the flag carried across the Red Square by leaders of the revolution on May Day, 1918. He designed propaganda posters, employing abstracted geometric forms appealing to Jews to support the Bolsheviks.

In 1919 Chagall invited Lissitzky to join the staff of the Art School in Vitebsk as Professor of Architecture and to head the Department of Applied Art. In Vitebsk, Lissitzky's work became increasingly abstract. This new abstraction culminated in Lissitzky's creation of *proun* (a Russian acronym for "projects affirming the new"), the merger of painting and architecture in nonobjective, geometric constructions.

This is one of ten illustrations from a portfolio by Lissitzky. Lissitzky's portfolio is unusual in that it illustrates the song *Had Gadya* ("One Kid") from the end of the seder service, yet is not related to the text of a haggadah. The verses of this song describe a goat who is consumed by a dog and continue to list a series of adversaries until finally God destroys the final assailant, the Angel of Death. In this scene, the stick is consumed by the flames of a fire-breathing rooster, illustrating the text "then came the fire and burnt the stick."

Lissitzky's composition combines various aspects of modern art vocabulary with Jewish folk art motifs. Illustrations of the *Had Gadya* text involve the depiction of animals, and zoomorphic motifs are a characteristic trait of European Jewish folk art. In this scene, Lissitzky has included the rooster, although it is not mentioned in this verse. The experimentation with Hebrew characters seen in the *Had Gadya* series is also found in Lissitzky's designs for Yiddish books.

Lissitzky created the *Had Gadya* series in 1919, the year of the Bolshevik victory. It has been suggested that he saw the *Had Gadya* as an allegory of survival and the ultimate triumph of Good over Evil, analogous to the victory of the Bolsheviks over the anti-Communist Whites. Lissitzky's work uses traditional themes and motifs and imbues them with modern stylistic approaches and contemporary political significance, indicating the timeless nature of the themes celebrated at Passover.

Colored lithograph on paper.
10 ¾ × 10 in. (27.3 × 25.4 cm).
The Jewish Museum, New York.
Gift of Leonard and Phyllis Greenberg.

Passover

1948

Arthur Szyk

Arthur Szyk (1894–1951) was born in Lodz, Poland. He spent a brief period in Paris after World War I and was in England at the beginning of World War II. By 1940 Szyk resided in New Canaan, Connecticut. A talented calligrapher and painter, his most famous works are a haggadah, produced during the early 1930s and published in 1940 and his decorative Declaration of Independence for the State of Israel. His works encompass designs for stained glass windows for synagogues and illustrations for non-Jewish books, including the fairy tales of Grimm and Andersen.

From 1940 to the end of World War II in 1945, Szyk produced political cartoons dealing with the Allied struggle and with the plight of the Jews fleeing the Nazis. Many of his cartoons appeared in *Colliers* and other prominent publications. During the Arab-Jewish conflict following the U.N. General Assembly decision on the partition of Israel adopted on November 29, 1947, Szyk continued to produce political cartoons dealing with the struggle for the survival of Israel.

The style of *Passover* remains unchanged from that of Szyk's haggadah illustrations of the 1930s; Szyk almost seems to shun any association with contemporary art and its painterly abstraction. His artistic antecedents stretch back to the detailed academic realism of the nineteenth century or the descriptive medieval manuscripts. We have the illusion of a three-dimensional reality existing beyond the surface of the paper, available to our view. Using jeweled colors and fine detail, Szyk produced an equivalent of elegant medieval manuscripts, showing a wealth of natural detail: the homes, clothing, pursuits, and possessions of the subject. There is some variation in the people's features, perhaps intended to heighten the illusion of realism; some could even be considered ugly.

The image offers its viewer a trip through time to the Poland of Szyk's past, a high watermark of culture, stability, family life, and religious strength. The work would appeal to the Jewish viewer's sense of tradition, of family values. It would have been viewed with nostalgia and bittersweet overtones by viewers still staggering from the horror of the Holocaust which had forever swept away all traces of the Polish *shtetl* along with a large percentage of its population.

Despite its apparent realism, this image represents the artist's private fantasy. The reality of the Polish *shtetl* was the opposite of the wealth needed to purchase luxury goods such as the fine silver and rich garments of Szyk's painting, or the plentitude suggested by the heaping platter of food.

Szyk appears to depict a specific moment of the Passover seder. In reality, he has combined two sections of the Passover seder that do not occur at the same time: the meal and the recitation of the Four Questions. By combining these two sections of the seder, Szyk summarizes the seder in a manner comprehensible to most people who would come in contact with his image. The recitation of the Four Questions by the youngest child and the meal are the two most memorable features of the seder and the most likely to signify all that is Passover.

Szyk's *Passover* is an image created purposefully, imparting a positive, if perhaps escapist, message to strengthen and inspire the Jewish people.

Tempera and ink on paper.
7 × 5 ½ in. (17.8 × 14 cm).
Yeshiva University Museum.
Gift of Mr. Charles Frost.

First Seder in Jerusalem

1950

Reuven Rubin

Reuven Rubin (1893–1974) was born in Romania. He studied in Europe and emigrated to Palestine in 1922. Rubin recognized that his bright, expressive colors and compositions paralleled the optimistic spirit of the early settlers in Israel and in 1926 he stated that "here in Jerusalem, Tel Aviv, Haifa, and Tiberias I feel myself reborn. Only here do I feel that life and nature are mine. The grey clouds of Europe have disappeared. . . . All is sunshine, clear light, and happy, creative work. As the desert revives and blooms under the hands of the pioneers, so do I feel awakening in me all the latent energies . . ." After the founding of the State of Israel, Rubin returned to Romania to serve as Israel's minister plenipotentiary. He spent eighteen months in Romania, during which time he helped to arrange exit permits for many Romanian Jews. When he returned to Israel, he sailed together with the first 1,000 of these Romanian emigrants.

The period following World War II saw tremendous pressure to establish Israel as an independent state, a homeland and refuge for Jews from around the world. Rubin was particularly moved by the arrival of so many Jews from so many backgrounds. In 1950 he painted *First Seder in Jerusalem*.

In this work he returned to the style of his earlier years. The scene shows a seder being conducted in Jerusalem. The walls of the Old City are visible through the arch on the right. The bearded man in the center, dressed in traditional Eastern European Hasidic garb, holds the seder plate. The woman standing behind him to the left holds a cup of wine. Several of the figures hold matzahs. Rubin is seated at the right embracing his son, his wife behind him. The group consists of figures representing the various Jewish communities.

The painting is strikingly reminiscent of Leonardo da Vinci's *The Last Supper*. The three open arches behind the table here are like the three open windows in da Vinci's work. Both paintings are composed symmetrically, with six adult figures to either side of the central figure. The white-robed man seated at the left of the table is quite striking. He holds his open hands with palms up, as did Jesus in *The Last Supper*. By portraying wounds on his hands and feet, Rubin leaves little doubt that this figure is Jesus. Perhaps the inclusion of the resurrected Jesus is to remind the world that the Jewish people also suffered and died but yet rose again to life in their own land. Rubin's title stands in contrast to da Vinci's—this is a *first* seder, not a *last* supper.

The inclusion of children reminds us of the biblical admonition to teach them the meaning of the Passover celebration. There is a dreamlike quality to the painting. Perhaps Rubin is suggesting that this peaceful scene is just a dream of a peaceful future that has not yet arrived, an impression strengthened by his portrayal of himself with his head resting on his hand, apparently lost in thought. Rubin used his art to construct a message of hope for a redeemed and renewed world in the aftermath of the destruction of the Holocaust.

Oil on canvas.
10 ½ × 64 in. (26.7 × 162.6 cm).
The Rubin Museum Foundation, Tel Aviv.

Exodus

1968

Marc Chagall

Marc Chagall (1887–1985) was born in the Russian-Jewish village of Vitebsk. Much of Chagall's fanciful imagery and brilliantly colored scenes derive from his childhood memories of life there. In 1922 Chagall and his wife Bella moved to France where he spent most of his life. In the 1940s, after the Nazis invaded France, he lived for a time in Mexico and the United States.

Chagall was one of the artists chosen to decorate the Knesset, the Israeli Parliament, in 1960. A pioneer of modern art and one of the foremost Jewish artists of his time, it was appropriate that he decorate this major monument to the Jewish people, a structure representing Jewish rule in the land of Israel for the first time in millenia.

Exodus is the largest of the set of three tapestries installed in the Knesset on June 18, 1969, and functions as the central panel. The other two represent the entry into Jerusalem of King David with the Ark and the prophecy of Isaiah. Reproducing Chagall's painted sketch in tapestry consisting of tiny stitches was a complicated undertaking involving the use of a color palette of 160 tones of thread and took three years to complete.

Exodus combines historical, religious, and sociopolitical elements. Slightly to the left of center, Moses leads the Jews out of Egypt. The coffin to the right contains the body of Joseph brought out of Egypt for burial in the Promised Land. Beyond is the worship of the golden calf and behind that a burning village, victim of a pogrom or the Holocaust.

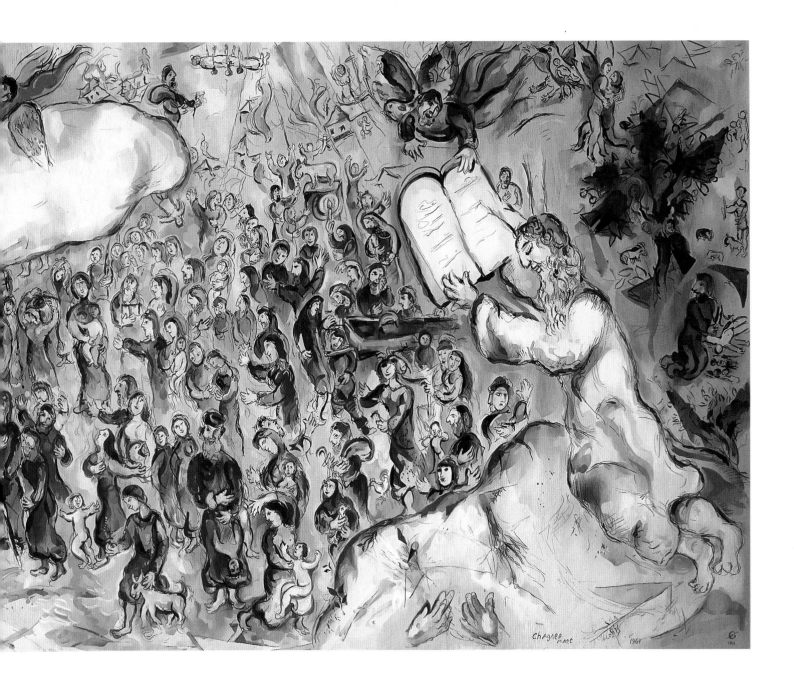

On the right, a monumental Moses receives the tablets inscribed with the Ten Commandements. Beyond are the sacrifice of Isaac and Jacob wrestling with the angel, representing the covenant between God and the Jewish people.

A heroic King David stands on the left; beyond him is a city labeled "Jerusalem." Opposite is a younger David, holding the head of the fallen Goliath who lies at his feet. The triumph of the small and weak over the great and mighty parallels that of the Jewish people, surviving and triumphing against its enemies to found the State of Israel.

Below Kind David is Aaron, representing the historical division of power in Israel—the High Priest and the secular King. It has been suggested that the bride recalls the prophecy of Jeremiah that the captivity of Israel will end and the voice of the bridegroom and the bride will be heard in the streets of Jerusalem (Jeremiah 33.7 and 33.11). The triumphal entry of the Jews into Jerusalem concludes the narrative.

Master Weaver: Mme. Bourbonneaux.
Gobelins tapestry, Manufacture Nationale des Gobelins, France.
187 × 208 in. (475 × 528 cm).
Knesset Building, Jerusalem.

Making Haroset

1975

Toby Knobel Fluek

Toby Knobel was born in Czernica, near Lvov, Poland. Before the Holocaust there were 250 families in the village—10 of whom were Jewish. During World War II Czernica was occupied twice, first by Soviet forces in 1939, and later by the Nazis in 1941. Under Nazi orders, the Knobel family was forced to leave their home and live in Brody.

A city in the Ukraine, Brody was part of Poland from 1919 until 1939. Jews of Brody were prominent in the diffusion of the *Haskalah* (Enlightenment) in Galicia during the nineteenth century. By the late 1930s the city had a population of over 10,000 Jews. The city had not had a ghetto since it was destroyed by fire in 1696; the Nazis established one in 1942 for the 6,500 surviving Jewish inhabitants of Brody and for refugees from neighboring towns, like the Knobels. This ghetto was sealed from outside contact. Shortages of food and fuel, in addition to typhoid fever, claimed hundreds of lives. Between September 19 and September 21, 1942, the Nazis began deporting the inhabitants to the Belzec death camp. Toby Knobel managed to escape the city in March 1943 as did one of her sisters. Not everyone was so fortunate. The 2,500 Jews who survived until May 1943 were deported to Maidanek.

Toby was able to hide from the Nazis, and her mother also managed to survive. One sister who had escaped Brody, another sister, her brother, and her father all perished in the Holocaust.

Knobel met her husband, Max Fluek, in a displaced persons camp; the Flueks and her mother emigrated to America. Toby Fluek helped her husband run a dry-cleaning business, painting during her spare time and studying at the Art Students League of New York. In the 1960s she began to confront both the peaceful and horrific episodes of her past in a series of paintings and sketches.

In this simple still life, the viewer is presented with the ingredients and tools used to prepare *haroset*—apples, wine, and nuts, a knife, a plain glass, and a brass mortar and pestle for grinding, standard equipment in the kitchens of Poland. The artist's father would grind the *haroset*, which the children were not allowed to taste until the seder.

In several respects, *Making Haroset* is a traditional work, part of the genre of still life, depictions of fruits, vegetables, and household utensils. Such subjects were depicted for various purposes throughout history. We find them in Egyptian tomb paintings, where they express the hope of the deceased for a life after death in which they will continue to enjoy the pleasures of the world. Still-life depictions have been excavated on walls in Pompeii and found decorating ancient mosaic floors. The height of popularity of the still life occurred in Holland during the seventeenth century.

While *Making Haroset* can be viewed simply as a depiction of items used for the preparation of this special Passover food, it can also represent relics of the way of life led by the artist in her childhood, a way of life destroyed along with members of her family during the Holocaust.

The subject of the composition is doubly suitable. *Haroset* is a delicious holiday treat, but it recalls the mortar used by the enslaved Israelites and the hardships they endured. *Making Haroset* also projects this dual, bittersweet nature. It simultaneously recalls Fluek's sweet life with her family before the Holocaust and the tragic losses sustained during the Nazi era.

Oil on canvas.
16 × 20 in. (40.6 × 50.8 cm).
Collection of the artist.

Part I—Before the Diaspora. 1982.

History of Matzah

1982–84   Larry Rivers

Larry Rivers was born Yitzroch Loiza Grossberg in 1923 in New York City, the only son of a Russian-Polish immigrant couple. He studied composition at the Juilliard School of Music and was a professional jazz saxophonist before turning to art.

In this three-part series, executed in acrylic on canvas, Rivers has given us a wonderful insight into the power of matzah as a symbol. Matzah stands for more than the Exodus from Egypt; it signifies the plight of the Jews through the ages, fleeing in haste from place to place in order to survive.

Rivers begins this triptych with the Israelites in Egypt, *Before the Diaspora,* continues with *European Jewry,* and concludes with the mass immigration of Jews to the United States in the early part of this century, *Immigration to America.* Multiple images from that history pass dreamlike before the eyes, superimposed over the matzah, giving the work the feeling of a montage—the dreamlike quality heightened by transparent washes of color. Some images derive from stories and sights familiar to the immigrant experience—for example, in the lower left corner of *Immigration to America,* one sees Rivers's interpretation of a well-known photograph of immigrants traveling in steerage. Other images are drawn from Renaissance art (Michelangelo's *David*) and cultural icons (the Statue of Liberty and portrait of Theodor Herzl).

Rivers paints from an Ashkenazic perspective. A Sefardic Jew might have portrayed scenes from such countries as Spain, Portugal, Holland, or Turkey.

By linking the symbol of matzah with the historical Jewish experience, Rivers presents the enduring power of a tradition and a people.

All paintings acrylic on canvas. Part I: 116 ¾ × 166 ½ in. (296.5 × 422.9 cm). Part II: 116 ¾ × 168 in. (296.5 × 426.7 cm). Part III: 116 ¼ × 180 in. (292.3 × 457.2 cm).
All Private Collection, New York. © Larry Rivers/VAGA, New York, 1993.

Part II–European Jewry. 1983.

Part III–Immigration to America. 1984.

Omer Calendar

Mid 19th Century, France
Maurice Mayer

The counting of the Omer is a ritual that begins on the second evening of Passover. The practice has its origin in the biblical command (Leviticus 23: 15–16) "And from the day on which you bring the sheaf of elevation offering—the day after the Sabbath—you shall count off seven weeks. They must be complete: you must count until the day after the seventh week —fifty days; then you shall bring an offering of new grain to the Lord." Thus forty-nine days are to be counted, and the day following the forty-ninth day shall be the holiday Shavuot, the Feast of Weeks. The command to observe Shavuot does not prescribe a month and day in that month for the celebration to take place; Shavuot is dependent on Passover. The word "Sabbath" in the phrase "The day after the Sabbath" has been understood in rabbinic literature to refer to the first day of Passover, which is a holy day, not to the Sabbath following the first day of Passover. Because the commandment refers to a count of both weeks and days, both are mentioned in the traditional formal count, for example: "Today is the twentieth day, which is two weeks and six days of the Omer." To help keep track of the count in its proper form, special Omer calendars were created.

The calendar shown here was made in the mid nineteenth century in France by Maurice Mayer, goldsmith to Napoleon III, emperor of France (1808–73). The case of this calendar is silver, partly gilt, adorned with coral pendants and semiprecious stones. The adjustable scroll in the case is painted parchment. The windows on the right-hand side contain the blessing recited before the count, a plea to God to rebuild the Temple in Jerusalem, and the order of the ritual. The center windows contain the actual count, here shown as the thirty-third day, four weeks and five days of the Omer. The windows on the left originally held labels for the three numbers. The "H" visible in the center window on the left should actually be in the topmost window, since it stands for "Homer," an alternate spelling for "Omer"; the next window should contain the letter "S" for "semanas" (weeks); the bottom window should contain the letter "D" for "dias" (days). The period of the Counting of the Omer culminates in Shavuot, the holiday celebrating the revelation of the Torah at Mount Sinai; the case is therefore crowned with the tablets containing the Ten Commandments.

This Omer calendar, like other Judaica crafted by Mayer, bears many stylistic characteristics typical of Second Empire decorative arts. The new empire sought to associate itself with earlier periods of grandeur, and objects were elaborately decorated with rococo ornaments and ornate repoussé. Maurice Mayer is known to have created elaborate Jewish ceremonial objects for the Sefardic community of France. An ornate silver *tik,* a rigid case for the Torah, was made by Mayer around 1860. The Spanish acronyms used here are also found in Omer calendars of the Western Sefardic communities of Amsterdam, London, and New York. Converso Sefardic exiles, living secretly as Jews, settled in Bayonne and Bordeaux soon after the expulsion of the Jews from Spain in 1492 and formed the nucleus of France's Sefardic community.

Glass; silver partly gilt; semi-precious stones; painted parchment.
13 ¾ × 10 ¼ × 3 in. (35 × 26 × 7.6 cm).
Hebrew Union College Skirball Museum, Los Angeles.

Index

Page numbers in *italics* denote illustrations.

Abbas I, Shah, 38
Adler, Friedrich, 78
Afikomen Pouch, 13, 58, *59*
Alexander the Great, 38
Alphabet of Creation, The (Shahn), 46
Alsace, France, 48, 52
Altman, Nathan, 100
Amsterdam Haggadah, 10, 40, 42, 86
Art Nouveau, 44, 78
Asher, R. Yaakov ben, 20
Ashkenazi Haggadah, 32, *33,* 36
Austria, 10, 74, 76
Avram bar Ya'akov, 10

Babylonian Talmud, 8, 38, 58
Barcelona, 22, 24
Barcelona Haggadah, 20, *21*
Bauhaus school, 78, 80
Bayazid II, Sultan, 96
Beaker, 86, *87*
Before the Diaspora (Rivers), *110*
Benguiat, Hadji Ephraim, 96
Benjamin of Tuldela, 48
Ben Shahn Haggadah, 46, *47*
Bezalel school, 44
Birds' Head Haggadah, The, 18, *19,* 28
Black Death, 20, 24, 48
Blümche, Abraham, 52
Bohemia, 40, 82, 92
Book of Exodus, 38, *39*
Books of Hours, 9, 26

Brass Seder Plate, 70, *71*
Bukovina, 76

Cairo *genizah,* 8
Caro, Yosef, 12
Catalonia, 24
Ceremonial Towel, 50, *51*
Cérémonies et coutumes religieuses de tous les peuples du monde, 98
Chagall, Marc, 14, 100, 106–107
China, 13, 58
Chronicles of the Aragonese King Jaime el Conquistador, 24
Code of Jewish Law, 12
Costa Athias, Solomon da, 32
Counting of the Omer, 112
Cup of Elijah, 13, 74, 78, *79,* 88, 92, *93, 94, 95*
Cup of Elijah (Schwartz), *94, 95*
Czechoslovakia, 64, 82

Danzig Jewish community, 72
Darmstadt Haggadah, 26, *27*
Debschitz School, 78
Die Welt, 76
Dura Europos synagogue, 8, *9,* 30
Duran, Profiat, 22

Eagle symbol, 76
Ehad Mi Yodea ("Who Knows One?"), 42
Elijah Cup, 13, 74, 78, *79,* 88, 92, *93, 94, 95*
Elijah Cup (Adler), 78, *79*
Embroidered Matzah Bags, 54, *55,* 60, *61*
Erna Michael Haggadah, 30, *31*
Ethics of the Fathers, 54

European Jewry (Rivers), 110, *111*
Ewer and Basin, 96, *97*
Exodus (Chagall), *106–107*

Fire Came and Burnt the Stick, The (Lissitzky), 100, *101*
First Seder in Jerusalem (Rubin), 104, *105*
Fischer, Moritz, 66
Fluek, Toby Knobel, 108–109
Food, 10, 12, 64, 76, 108
Forgeries, 68
Four Sons, 86

Galicia, 76, 108
Gansmann, Isaac ben Simhah, 28
Genre painting, 98
Germany, 9, 10, 18, 26, 28, 30, 32, 52, 56, 86, 90, 92
Glass Goblets, 92, *93*
Glassmaking, 92
Goblets, 88, *89,* 92, *93*
Golden Age of Jewish Spain, 62
Golden Haggadah, 18, 22, *23*
Gropius, Walter, 78, 80
Gruss, Alex, 14, 84–85
Gruss, Lorelei, 14, 84–85
Gur-Arieh, Meir, 44

Had Gadya ("One Kid"), 42, 52, 70, 100
Hamburg Miscellany, 28, *29*
Harley, Robert, Earl of Oxford, 32
Haroset, 12, 76, 108
Haskalah (Enlightenment) movement, 76, 108
Herend, Hungary, 14, 66
Herzl, Theodore, 76, 110

Hiddur mitzvah, 7, 8, 14, 56
History of Matzah (Rivers), 14, *110–111*
Hitler, Adolf, 80
Hofjude (Court Jew), 40, 42
Holocaust, 14, 40, 102, 104, 108
Hungary, 54, 66, 76

Icones Biblicae (Merian), 86
Immigration to America (Rivers), 110, *111*
Industrial Revolution, 92
Inlaid ceremonial art, 84, *85*
International Gothic, 26
Iran, 38
Israel, 14, 44, 104
Israelites Crossing the Red Sea (wall painting), *9*
Istanbul, 96
Italy, 9, 34, 36, 68
Ivory, 90
Ivory Beaker, 90, *91*

Jerusalem, 70
Jewish Museum of New York, 96
Jewish Theological Seminary, 96
Judah of Worms, Eleazar ben, 32
Judenstern (hanging lamp), 30, 32
Jugendstil idiom, 44, 78

Kinot (memorial prayers), 28
Kirchmayr, C., 68
Knesset, 106
Korban Pesach, 64

Last Supper (Leonardo da Vinci), 34, 104

Leonardo da Vinci, 34, 104
Leusden, Johann, 98
Lion symbol, 50
Lissitzky, El, 14, 100-101
Little Office of Our Lady, 26
Lusterware, 14, 62
Lusterware Passover Plate, 62, *63*

Mahmoud II, Sultan, 96
Majolica Seder Plate, 68, *69*
Making Haroset (Fluek), 108, *109*
Mamluk revival, 70
Mantua Haggadah, 10
Matthathias, Jacob, 32
Matzah Bag, 56, *57*
Matzah bags, 13, 54, *55,* 56, *57,* 58, *59,* 60, *61*
Mayer, Maurice, 112–113
Meir, Israel ben, 26
Meissen porcelain, 66
Merian, Matthew, 10, 86
Meshal ha-Kadmoni (animal fables), 34
Michelangelo, 10, 34
Midrash, 86
Miniature Haggadah, 42, *43*
Mona Lisa (Leonardo da Vinci), 34
Moravia, 10, 40, 60, 82
Moses, Natan, 54
Muhammad, 38

Nathan, 40
Nebuchadnezzar, 20, 38

Needlework, 50, *51, 52, 53,* 54, *55,* 56, *57,* 58, *59,*
   60, *61*
Northwood, John, 92

Omer Calendar (Mayer), 112, *113*
Oppenheim, Moritz, 14, 15, 66, 92
Ottoman Empire, 70, 96

Paschal lamb, 13, 52
Passover (Szyk), 102, *103*
Passover Banner, 48, *49*
Passover Plates, 66, *67*
Passover plates, 62, *63,* 64, *65,* 66, *67*
Passover Roundels, 36, *37*
Passover Scenes from Old Jewish Family Life
   (Oppenheim), 14, *15*
Persia, 38
Pewter, 14, 64
Pewter Passover Plate, 64, *65*
Philologus Hebraeo Mixtus (Leusden), 98
Picart, Bernard, 14, 98–99
Pillows, 12, 50, 56
Poland, 54, 72, 88, 102, 108
Porcelain, 66
Pottery, 62
Prague, 10, 64
Prague Haggadah, 40, *41*
Printing, invention of, 9, 10

Raban Haggadah, 44, *45*
Raban, Zeev, 14, 44–45

Rashi, Rabbi Solomon ben Isaac, 54
Repoussé Tiered Seder Plate, 76, 77
Ritual washing of hands, 48, 50, 52, 96
Rivers, Larry, 14, 110–111
Romania, 54, 60, 104
Rosenberg, Pauline, 60
Rothschild Miscellany, 34, 35, 36
Rubin, Reuven, 14, 104-105
Ryback, Issachar, 100
Rylands Sefardic Haggadah, 24, 25

Schatz, Boris, 44
Schneerson, Menachem M., 94
Schwartz, Michel, 94–95
Search for Leaven/L'Examen du Levain (Picart), 98, 99
Seder Plate (Wörle), 80, 81
Seder plates, 12, 13, 68, 69, 70, 71, 72, 73, 74, 75, 76,
    77, 78, 79, 80, 81, 82, 83, 84, 85
Seder Towel, 52, 53
Sèvres porcelain, 66
Shahin, 38
Shahn, Ben, 14, 46–47
Sharif, Ahmad Pasha Karim ibn, 96
Shavuot, 112
Shulhan Arukh (Code of Jewish Law), 12
Silver Gilt Goblet, 88, 89
Silver Tiered Seder Plate, 74, 75
Simeon, Joel ben, 9, 32
Sistine Chapel ceiling, 10, 34
Sixtus V, Pope, 22
Sofer, Rabbi Moses, 74
Spain, 9, 18, 20, 22, 24, 62

Still life, 108
Szyk, Arthur, 102–103

Terezín (Theresienstadt), 82
Terezín Seder Plate, 7, 13, 82, 83
Tiered Seder Plate and Elijah Cup (Adler), 78, 79
Tiered Seder Plate: From Slavery to Freedom
    (Lorelei and Alex Gruss), 84, 85
Tiered Seder Set, 72, 73
Tin-glazed earthenware, 68
Tombac, 96
Towels, 12, 48, 49, 50, 51, 52, 53, 56
Turkey, 96

Utensils, 10, 12

Venice Haggadah, 10, 11, 42, 66, 88
Vienna Genesis, 90
Viennese seder plates, 74, 75, 76, 77

Warsaw, 88
Weimar Republic, 80
Wörle, Alois, 80–81

Yitzhak, Schlomo ben, 20
Yitzhak, Yosef ben, 90

Zionism, 44, 76

Photo Credits